ASPECTS OF BRADFORD 2

ASPECTS *of* BRADFORD

DISCOVERING LOCAL HISTORY

Edited by
Bob Duckett

Series Editor
Brian Elliott

Wharncliffe Books

First Published in 2000 by
Wharncliffe Books
an imprint of
Pen and Sword Books Limited,
47 Church Street, Barnsley,
South Yorkshire. S70 2AS

*For up-to-date information on other titles produced under the
Wharncliffe imprint, please telephone or write to:*

> **Wharncliffe Books**
> **FREEPOST**
> **47 Church Street**
> **Barnsley**
> **South Yorkshire S70 2BR**
> **Telephone (24 hours): 01226 - 734555**

ISBN: 1-871647-82-7

A CIP catalogue record of this book is available from the
British Library

Cover illustration: Manningham Mills, Bradford.
Tim Smith, Bradford Heritage Recording Unit

Printed in Great Britain by
Redwood Books, Trowbridge, Wiltshire

CONTENTS

INTRODUCTION

by Bob Duckett

Quite by chance many of the contributions to this second *Aspects of Bradford* focus on health – always, it seems, a topic of interest and concern. Even before the awful social conditions of the Industrial Revolution, man's hold on life was ever tenuous. Local historian, Elvira Willmott gives us a glimpse of everyday life in mid-eighteenth century Bradford when life was ever a battle. Graphic testimony to the losers comes from Ann Dinsdale, whose office at the Brontë Parsonage Museum overlooks the much-visited churchyard at Haworth. What poignant and heartrending stories lie beyond the inscriptions on the graves and memorial stones! What an unhealthy place was Haworth!

Efforts to improve public health pioneered by The Reverend Brontë and others hit an obstacle down the hill in Keighley. Here, many of the town's guardians objected to the compulsory vaccination of children and, in the cause of personal liberty, went to prison for their belief. This forgotten story, unearthed by reference librarian Pauline Barfield, has resonance today. And if you did go to hospital, well, let's hope your friends and relations kept you well supplied with food! Christine Alvin tells of the patient's lot in the days when the Bradford Infirmary was in Westgate. For the rich, such as Charles Darwin, there was always hydrotherapy at Ilkley. Teacher Pat Brown was a student at the College of Domestic Science which opened in the very hotel which had earlier offered hydrotherapy. The raising of domestic standards was a priority in those postwar years.

Schooldays contribute to mental health, don't they? That well-known authority on dialect, Arnold Kellett, seems to have enjoyed his school days at Carlton. Glimpses of other people's early lives are always fascinating, particularly of public figures. Retired engineer, David Hird, is less sure about his school days, though his childhood in Great Horton was benign and memorable, and beautifully recorded. Those gloves on elastic! Those third-pint bottles of milk!

Religion, literature, leisure and beer, are also part of our heritage. The Methodist legacy is all around us, and teacher and lay preacher, Simon Valentine, tells us how it got there, and who the early pioneers were. Lecturer Stephen Wade introduces us to the journalist James

Burnley, one of the more active of those writers in the late Victorian flowering of culture in Bradford. James Burnley's *Saunterer's Satchel* was a hugely popular magazine of its time. Flowers of a real kind are a focus of Peter Shutt's article. He looks back nostalgically to the many pleasures enjoyed at Lister Park, from bandstands, boating and bathing, to the exhibitions, parading, and flowers.

Finally, there is beer, and Henry L. Bradfer-Lewis. Tony Avis came from rural Norfolk to be Company Secretary at Hammond's Fountain Brewery on the Manchester Road. He experienced one of the last of the great authoritarian company directors. His account will interest students of management, those who remember the Bradford of the 1950s, and drinkers of beer!

I would like to thank all of those who gave me freely of their material. My apologies to those whose material I did not use, but the success that Wharncliffe Books has had leads me to anticipate *Aspects of Bradford 3*, so maybe I can use it then. Keep the contributions flowing in. Keep our past alive!

I can be found in the Reference Library at Bradford, or you can contact the publishers. My particular thanks go to Mick Birdsall for his disc management skills, to Peter Walker for compiling the index, to Tim Smith for the striking cover photograph, and to Mike Parsons and his colleagues at Wharncliffe for their patience and their skill.

1. Random Reverie: Memories of an Impressionable Child

by David Hird

PERHAPS I WAS ALWAYS AN IMPRESSIONABLE CHILD, for selected childhood memories are with me still, half a century later. I can clearly remember severe localised flooding following the heavy snowfalls of 1947's winter and being carried across Town Hall Square, at the age of two. That feat of recollection is topped by a somewhat precocious sister able to picture clearly a visit to a particular Victorian villa and to describe in some considerable detail its internal arrangements and decor; the twist is that this property was at the time that of a medical practitioner specialising in pre-natal treatment. My sister had not then been born, and the building was never visited again by any family member (Figure 1).

Figure 1. Victorian villa, Little Horton Lane, the scene of my sister's prodigious feat of pre-natal recall. *D.M. Hird*

The adult world is always a strange and perhaps forbidding place to a young child, but humour, or humorous memories of humorous incidents, always shines throughout one's consciousness. I recall clearly the visit of a friend of my father who carried his fishing rods wrapped in a voluminous black hessian bag. I was convinced that this man was God's agent on earth and that every night, without fail, he unrolled the bag across the sky to provoke the onset of the night. He must also have retrieved the covering early next morning when everyone was still asleep, because no-one ever reported his ritual activities, at least not within my hearing, I was absolutely convinced that this was so. At some time in my later childhood or early adolescence it struck me with some force that my conviction was a self-delusion born of an over-active imagination or an irrational fear of black hessian, or both. I kept it to myself, however, and chuckled quietly at the memory, and still do.

One source of confusion to an alert child is vocabulary beyond comprehension. It always caused considerable concern to my then tender sensibilities when adults were overheard discussing the Eye and Ear Hospital; what possessed willing patients to submit themselves to the indignity of being fitted with ferrous auditory equipment left me worried, but again not outwardly so. And yet again, when realisation dawned, much secret hilarity was engendered, embarrassment ensuring that private mirth remained private.

Surely I could not have been the only child at that time convinced that Sinatra's rival in the American crooning stakes laboured under the name of Victor Moan?

And imagine what great but slightly dubious pleasure was derived from the advertising slogan developed from the manufacturer's initials proudly displayed on the delivery lorry's tailboard, that it was positively beneficial to drink T and P table waters.

Yet another impression clearly imprinted on my childhood memories is the occasion of the skilled painter and decorator attending to the internal doors in our home. Oil Scumble was the medium employed and the treatment involved the decorator wrapping a penny piece in a rag and then marking a representation of woodgrain into the still wet surface. I watched with increasing fascination at this all too obvious and amazing craftsmanship. In mid-process the decorator paused and, turning towards me in his white overalls bearing the evidence of innumerable past successes, lectured me with all the seriousness he could muster upon the great secrecy of the technique in which he was engaged. He almost pleaded with me to keep his secret and never to divulge it to anyone. I never did. It just did not occur to me that all over the country there were probably hundreds of other youngsters carrying on their formative years under this and similar unlikely but nevertheless onerous burdens. And, of course, when realisation was finally accepted that the secret was really a universally known truth, it simultaneously became obvious that the only way to avoid ridicule among one's peers was to suffer (or enjoy) the joke in silence. Now that really was a secret.

Memories of early childhood friends remain subliminally deep, to be triggered into recollection by unknown and unexpected moments; of Dennis Smith and getting trapped under his Dad's enormous iron bike whilst playing in the shed, and being quite unable to escape despite the earnest attentions of all the neighbourhood's wiry but worried contemporaries, fearful of an adverse adult reaction; of Billy Sharratt who was perpetually building wheeled contrivances from old boards and pram wheels - always an endless supply - but never having a drill bit with which to fashion the steering pivot, finally resorting to making the hole with a red hot poker and incinerating the entire magnificent structure when within grasp of completion; of Elva Morgan with the tight dark wringlets and no other memory; of Christine Fieldhouse, for whom I carried a secret indefinable sensation which much later I realised was the very beginnings of lust but, alas,

Figure 2. Christine Fieldhouse, author's sister, and the author at Quaker Lane. The age of innocence, when the sun always shone. *D.M. Hird*

was by then accepted as libido with lethargy; of Stuart Ellis who had the first television set for what seemed miles around and who also had the largest coterie of friends during Children's Hour; and of Derrick Moore, of whom 1 can recall nothing but the name (Figure 2).

Irene Marshall, a couple or so years older than I, was paid sixpence (2.5p) a week to see me safely to school. It was not until several years later that a certain unease developed in me with the realisation that I never actually heard a safe return journey mentioned as part of the remuneration. I suppose the inference was there, but subtleties of that nature escape all but the keenest of youthful intellects.

The corner shop was always a great source of wonderment, a part of the real adult world it was possible to penetrate without the risk of admonishment. The image it recalls is one of darkness, and towering timber shelves stacked with not very much in those days of the late 1940s, of produce in sacks on the floor - large earth-covered potatoes and carrots, onions in green net, limp cabbages, dried peas - a scrubbed board floor with its very own smell never encountered elsewhere, bulk sugar and butter in soft blue paper wrapping to be weighed out on demand, donkey stone, yellow stone and white stone, mop heads which seemed permanent fixtures high in the ceiling as none, apparently, was ever sold, and lentils in a sack on the counter. At this time lentils exerted a particular fascination for me. Mother never used them or sent me for them. There they sat, urging me in their orange attractiveness to buy. I convinced myself that they must be the most luscious comestible on offer in the entire establishment; everyone else appeared to use them and, for all I knew, to enjoy their foreign delights wholeheartedly. I could no longer resist their blandishments and, having saved a few coppers, asked for some 'for the soup'. On the way home I started munching on them. Never has such an overwhelming sense of disappointment, betrayal, unfulfilment, entrapment, enticement and treachery been contained within a tiny vegetable disc. I found it unbelievable how it was possible for a beguiling treat, in the instant of purchase and long-desired ownership, to transform into an indigestible substance with all the chewability of builders' sand. It was a defining moment in my life. Lentils even now hold no seductive charm for me.

It is beyond dispute that in those far off days the corner shop was often the first rung in the ladder of education. I can clearly recall my own delight and sense of achievement and personal pride having decoded the bleach bottle label. Bleach was sold under the trade name LANRY, an unusual, exotic device I thought, until inspiration in my formative powers of deduction enlightened me; the manufacturers were Allan and Harry Brown and the name came from the last syllables of each partner's first name. Simple really, but powerful medicine to an enquiring mind.

Just around from the corner shop lived a Mrs Cullen, just a regular run-of-the-mill old lady but her dog was something else. I recall it as being a somewhat overweight bull terrier, albino white with searing red eyes, canine halitosis and truncated legs as though cloned from a leather-topped foot stool. Every child in the neighbourhood was convinced that the dog was a reincarnation of some evil forbear with strange powers, and therefore Mrs Cullen must be the last remaining witch in England. We were all terrified of looking the dog in the eyes, for in that way it would achieve supremacy over our souls, whatever that meant, but it certainly could not be good for you. We all spent the whole of one summer each armed with a coloured sweet wrapper through which to peer with half closed eyes at the dog should we ever meet, thus effectively countering its occult powers. How do you explain that to an adult who does not appreciate the complexities of a childhood imagination?

Another old lady nearby lived in a large detached house with rambling and unkempt gardens. Nothing remarkable in that, except that the house had leaded windows with richly coloured and multi-faceted glass which caught the sunlight in an awe-inspiring way. This, allied to the glass bead curtains hanging in every doorway throughout the house, had us absolutely convinced that here was a person of immense wealth, for did she not own every precious jewel on earth and was she not unafraid of displaying them? The house and its occupant always evoked a tremendous sense of reverence in us, even before we knew what reverence was.

Imagination itself provides access into strange worlds denied young minds. Surely everyone now remembers the effort expended striving to see over the fish shop counter, hitherto a mysterious ambiance of sounds and smells; and the intense disappointment on achieving the requisite vertical development, when all you saw was yet another shopkeeper keeping one eye on his assistants and the other on the till.

Other childhood memories which fleetingly emerge, unbidden, are the smell of fresh home-baked bread placed on the hearth of a neighbouring 'aunt'. We always used shop-bought bread in those days before the pre-wrapped and pre-sliced era, alas without the delicious aroma. 'Auntie' Ruth asked for and was given my favourite drawing-pin with which to secure a loose corner of heavily embossed wallpaper, when the drawing-pin was a whole new exciting treasure for me and one which I had kept safe and secret for what seemed ages. I could almost taste the sense of loss. The coalman was a dark (inevitably) visitor whom I was requested to scrutinise in the performance of his every move. The strategy was to count the sacks as they were upended into the coal chute and to make sure every one ordered was delivered. He knew that I was counting, and I knew that he knew that I was watching and counting. But he did not know that my counting was not the most accurate, and that whatever happened during this clandestine cat-and-mouse game I would later report that all was in order. Why argue with a coalman, tall as a giant and featureless apart from his eyes and lips and in possession of more coal than anyone could possibly ever need?

Mittens linked with a length of elastic also conjure strong reactions when the memory races across the adult retrieval system. The elastic ran across the shoulders and down the sleeves ensuring that neither mitten was lost individually or that both were lost together. What usually happened was that having inserted the hand into one mitt it then became impossible to insert the other because of the strength of the linking elastic. This obliged you to conduct the remainder of your day's excitement with one frozen hand and a lump on the opposing bicep (Figure 3). Every child was invariably instructed to put on a coat or jumper when going outdoors, otherwise 'you will not feel the benefit'. What was all this about benefit? You put on a coat. You play out. You find mud. You fall in it. You go home. You get shouted at. Where is the benefit in that, and to whom does the benefit accrue? Strange people, adults!

Referring to winter protection

Figure 3. Author and sister in Sunday best at the steps of the old Kirkgate Market. This photograph provides incontrovertible proof that gloves were worn with a length of elastic across the shoulders. *D.M. Hird*

for the hands brings back memories of thick woollen gloves caked in solid snow and the distinctive, unique almost, taste they produced. Who could resist the temptation to suck snow from those gloves? I remember excessive pride in my first pair of brown allegedly leather gloves, and the uproar caused when helping unofficially with a newspaper delivery round as the colour leeched from them and made the evening editions reminiscent of the wrapping from fresh liver. Some days start off bad and just get worse.

And how was it always possible for milk to completely change character with the seasons? Remember those tiny one-third of a pint bottles issued at primary school which, having been thawed next to the heating pipes in winter, dispensed milk separated into globs of solids floating on grey liquid, or thick slightly odorous gloop presented in summer when the crates had been carefully stacked in the sun for half a day?

One abiding memory from grammar school days is that of being a member of a class of young boys instructed at the end of every woodwork lesson to 'stand by your vices'. I have always tried to comply with this sincere command, although my vices have developed - one might even use the term 'refined' - with the inevitable passage of time, and I cannot now afford most of them.

Everyone has memories of childhood, some fond and some not so fond. It was invariably a time when the sun shone all year through except for those two or three days in winter when the snow remained clean and crisp; snow never went slushy, and it departed just as swiftly as it appeared. Childhood is a time of absolutes - no half measures, black or white, all in glorious living full colour.

I recently revisited, after a lapse of almost half a century, the streets which encompassed these memories. The immediate reaction is how much smaller everything appears, and how what seemed to be immense distances at that impressionable age are now of little consequence. The impressive Victorian villa in Little Horton Lane which was the scene of my sister's prodigious feat of memory remains, much as remembered, but in a sadly delapidated condition and suffering from the ravages of neglect. Alas the house of my infancy, 32 Quaker Lane, Little Horton, and the corner shop which provoked those deeply etched influences are no more; both have succumbed to the inevitable march of progress and enhanced housing and shopping aspirations. Not for the first time in this exercise in memory dredging, the site is now occupied by what appears to be a typically anonymous local authority sheltered housing complex, devoid of all character and charisma (Figure 4).

Figure 4. Modern housing complex on the site of 32 Quaker Lane, Little Horton, and the evocative corner shop. *D.M. Hird*

Figure 5. Old cottages, Quaker Lane, Little Horton. The tall house mid-foreground contained those brilliant stained glass and bead curtains. *D.M. Hird*

Quaker Lane took its name from the selection of a site along its length by early members of the Bradford Society of Friends as a burial ground. Interments commenced in 1656 with one Thomas Judson and ended in 1699 with Paul, son of John Harwood of Bradford, Edward Wood of Great Horton and John Appleyard the Elder of Bowling (Figure 5).

Rows of ancient single storey cottages along Southfield Lane have survived much as I remember them, clearly owner-occupier cherished and nurtured despite the road-wideners' ambitions. My grandparents lived, during my very early years, nearby in Haycliffe Road. A visit there, always on foot and usually on a Sunday afternoon, was ever an eagerly anticipated excursion. It was an outing to be savoured, and guaranteed a homeward journey full of jelly (always made with rather less boiling water than recommended and, consequently, with the consistency of cushion foam) and fancy buns. The Sunday afternoon tea even now carries clear connotations of stinging behind the knees - the uncut moquette grandparental couch was torture to short legs not yet benefiting from long-trousered bliss. The Haycliffe Road house remains, but somehow it is much closer now to the Quaker Lane home in which I grew up.

I was in those days a pupil at what we all knew as Bell School, but which was actually named - if my memory is reasonably accurate - Southfield Lane Primary School (Figure 6). How fortunate I was in

Figure 6. The former Southfield Lane Primary School, Great Horton. *D.M. Hird*

those far off days to have escaped being labelled a 'Junior Mixed Infant'. However the Bell Chapel, from which my former school borrowed its name, evokes visions of a rather dark, dour, *Wuthering Heights* type Brontë-esque foursquare building of black ashlar blocks devoid of all decoration and surrounded by a brooding graveyard. The old Bell Chapel was erected between 1806 and 1808 and consecrated on 1 July 1809 as a chapel of ease to the Parish Church (later Cathedral) of Bradford. The whole of the building cost of £1,200 was raised by local subscription. The original Bell School was opened alongside in 1861 and the Bell Chapel later still converted to infant school use following the consecration of the new Great Horton St John's Church in 1874.

The Bell Chapel memories are reasonably accurate; it is still brooding, and gothic, and somewhat forbidding, although the headstones are now removed, more in keeping, perhaps, with its present incarnation as a retail tile warehouse (Figure 7).

The school itself now serves as a retirement home. There we have my life encapsulated; from the cradle (almost) to the grave (almost).

I remember also the delicious, almost risqué, delights of the travelling fair which visited the plot adjacent to Bell School once or twice a year. The land on which the fair was sited was always known by my generation as 'the Tide Field', 'tide' being a coloquiallism for

Figure 7. Bell Chapel, Southfield Lane, Great Horton. Note the gravestones now serving as a boundary wall. *D.M. Hird*

Figure 8. Modern housing on the site of Great Horton 'Tide Field'. *D.M. Hird*

fair. And 'field' is a great exaggeration; the land was just a patch of bare shale and scrubby weeds. Well, there was Horton Tide, and Wibsey Tide and, of course Bowling Tide, familiar to a much wider body of Bradfordians, for it extended to a week and invariably accompanied an annual holiday when the local mills closed.

Alas, the Tide Field is no more. It now supports a dreadful mid-Elizabethan brick creation masquerading as speciously genteel accommodation for the elderly, an ideal accompaniment to the granny farm next door (Figure 8). I cannot help thinking that any one of its residents would gladly exchange one day's hilarity at Horton Tide for a month's enforced regimented existence in the present eventide establishment.

Hey ho! This is now what we are obliged to regard as progress.

2. LIFE IN MID-EIGHTEENTH CENTURY BRADFORD

by Elvira Willmott

MID-EIGHTEENTH CENTURY BRADFORD was a rapidly growing township with a population of perhaps two and a half thousand, twice as large as the combined total of the three adjoining townships of Bowling, Horton and Manningham, but only about a fifth of the size of Leeds. Situated where three valleys meet, Bradford was at a natural crossing point of Bradford beck; its three main streets of Ivegate, Kirkgate and Westgate were on the west bank of the beck, across which Ive (or Sun) bridge led to scattered houses near the Turles (the present City Hall area), and the church bridge led to the parish church and a few houses at the beginning of the road to Leeds (Figure 1).

A drawing of Bradford in 1718/9 shows a cluster of houses descending into the valley of the beck, with the manor hall in

Figure 1. View of Bradford from the south. *John Warburton 1718/9*, S.O. Bailey, Plans of Bradford, Bradford Antiquary, Vol. 4. 1905, opp p.225.

The South Prospect of Bradford

Kirkgate standing up above the roofs on one side and the parish church similarly prominent on the other, less populated, side. The houses were mostly built of stone, some of them small and single-storeyed, but others substantial with two, and occasionally three, storeys and several rooms on each floor. Probate inventories (lists of possessions made after the deaths of some of the Bradford men and women whose wills were proved in the 1740s and 1750s) list the spits, jacks, tongs, pokers etc. to be found in every home. They all contained at least a bed and bedding, a table and a chair, and a limited number of pots and pans. But in some houses there were dressers, settles, pewter dishes, cutlery and a wide range of cooking implements such as frying pans, chopping knives, and saucepans, as well as, perhaps, a tea kettle, a mustard box or tart tins. Also to be found in the houses of some of the wealthier Bradfordians were easy chairs, cushions, curtains, pictures, mirrors, clocks, and silver spoons, mugs and salt cellars.[1]

There was considerable numbers of masons living in Bradford at this time, and they, together with the smaller number of plasterers, joiners, carpenters and glaziers in the township, were probably able to construct and repair most of the houses, as well as make much of the furniture which they contained. Several clockmakers and a watchmaker were also working in Bradford, but those who could afford luxury goods probably obtained them from Leeds which was developing into a regional centre.[2]

Food was not listed in the inventories, except for one reference to a meal ark (a lidded bin for keeping grain, usually not wheat, after it had been ground) and its contents, but ale was mentioned several times, as were mash tubs (vats in which malt and boiling water were placed in the first stage of brewing). Ale would have been the daily drink at the time. Bradford's first water company was formed in 1744. Water from Haycliffe Hill, Little Horton, was conveyed in wooden pipes to Holme Top, and from there in lead pipes to a cistern at the top of Westgate with a capacity of about 15,000 gallons. Here it was supposed to be available for one hour each day, but was frequently only available for half an hour on three days a week.[3]

Everyone in Bradford living within two miles of the Bradford Soke Mill was legally required to have their corn, grain and malt ground there, and it was forbidden for any other mills to be set up. A charge was made for the grinding: in the 1740s it was $1/16$th part of all wheat ground, $1/24$th part of oats and about $1/45$th of malt. But there were other mills in the vicinity which were frequented by people who claimed that there was often insufficient water at the Bradford mill to

Figure 2. The old Soke Mill, nineteenth century drawing. *William Scruton's Scrapbook 83, p. 49.*

grind all the corn taken there[4] (Figure 2).

It is unlikely that Bradford was self-sufficient in the production of food. Most of the land in Bradford and the immediately surrounding area is between 300 and 600 hundred feet above sea level, and poor soil and an uncooperative climate have always made agriculture difficult.[5] Daniel Defoe writing in the 1720s about the West Riding said that the area around Halifax was supplied with corn from Lincoln, Nottingham and the East Riding, butter from the East and North Ridings, cheese from Cheshire and Warwickshire, and sheep from adjacent counties.[6] Bradford probably obtained some of its food from the same places.

Few local men were employed solely in farming in the mid-eighteenth century, although some would have combined agriculture with another occupation. According to Defoe:

Every clothier must keep a horse, perhaps two, to fetch and carry for the use of his manufacture, (viz.) to fetch home his wool and his provisions from the market, to carry his yarn to the spinners, his manufacture to the fulling mill, and, when finished, to the market to be sold, and the like; so every manufacturer generally keeps a cow or two, or more, for his family.

A few of the Bradford inventories list a horse, cows or a pig.

But there was some arable farming in Bradford and Horton as was shown when the barns of two farmers from these places were burnt down on successive nights in December 1759. They both petitioned the Quarter Sessions for money to replace the barns and their contents, one asking for £66 to erect a new barn and £36 10s (£36.50p) to replace the wheat, oats and hay burnt in the old one, and the other asking for £99 10s (£99.50p) to make his barn good, £3 for husbandry gears and £80 5s (£80.25) to replace his wheat, oats, barley, hay and lintels.[7] Cattle fairs were also held annually in Horton at this time.

Bradford was well supplied with butchers, and there was a number of bakers and grocers. Millers, maltsters and salters also worked in the town, and there were at least twenty innkeepers. Eighteenth century inns were often more than places providing food, drink and accommodation. They could be centres of commercial, administrative and social activity with trading facilities such as storage. They were often places where local justices and parish officials held their meetings, proving especially important when elections were held, as well as being convenient for public events.[8]

Clothing workers in the middle of the century included a considerable number of shoemakers and tailors, as well as hatters, a few glovers, some breeches makers and a clogger. The large numbers of some of these workers make it seem likely that they were producing footwear and clothing for people living beyond the Bradford boundaries.

Among the other occupations represented in the town was a considerable number of nail makers, with their associated wire drawers, and fellmongers, skinners, tanners, curriers and saddlers, all connected with the use of leather. Like the saddlers, blacksmiths showed the importance of horses in the local economy. There was also a number of whitesmiths (who worked with tin) coopers, ropers, coalminers, and a number of labourers whose precise jobs are unknown.

The largest category of workers, however, was connected with the

Figure 3. Manor Hall, Kirkgate. Nineteenth century drawing. *William Scruton's Scrapbook* 83, p.44.

wool textile industry. The numbers of such men in Bradford probably grew from about 20 per cent of all male workers in 1710 to nearly 50 per cent in 1780, and to them should be added the women and children who worked with them. During the same period the proportion of those producing worsted goods, rather than woollen goods, changed from about 10 per cent to about 75 per cent, with younger men probably changing to worsted sooner than their older companions. In neighbouring Bowling, Horton and Manningham slightly higher proportions of men were engaged in textile work, and the change from wool to worsted probably came earlier.

Providers of services were represented in Bradford by carters and carriers, gardeners, tobacconists, barbers and a variety of shopkeepers, including a hardwareman, a bookseller and stationer. More surprising was the presence of a musician and of a dancing master. There were also a number of apothecaries, bailiffs, excise officers, attorneys, schoolmasters and clergymen, as well as members of the gentry, some of whom probably overlapped with the top layers of other occupations. Servants and soldiers (the Seven Years' War was being fought between 1756 and 1763) made up the other main categories of occupations.

Although comparatively small, and with communications which only improved slowly as the century progressed, Bradford had a market and was the centre of a large and scattered parish (in which the chapelries of Haworth, Thornton and Wibsey had been established during the previous century). Thus, as well as coming to church for the Sunday services, parishioners would have come to Bradford for the weekly market (established in 1251) held at this time at the bottom of Westgate, for the fairs held each year, or to attend the manorial courts. It is also noticeable that Bradford contained a much greater number of specialised occupations than neighbouring Bowling, Horton and Manningham, and that it was clearly the pre-eminent township.

There were a number of links with the wider world outside Bradford Dale. The production of textiles was already important, and as local sheep were unable to provide sufficient wool for the growing industry it was obtained from many other parts of the country, especially Leicestershire and Lincolnshire. The wool was usually brought to Wakefield or Leeds by water, and transported from there by road. The iron required by the local nail makers almost certainly came from Kirkstall Forge, three miles north-west of Leeds. The parish register of 1720 mentions a London carrier, living in Bowling, who probably formed part of a network of carriers linking all parts of the kingdom with London and with each other. When Ivebridge required repair in 1741 it was described as 'standing in a great high road between London and Kendall and other parts of Westmorland'.[9]

Although some administrative matters were dealt with locally, Bradford men were involved in affairs at county level. The West Riding Quarter Sessions met at Pontefract each Easter, and the Midsummer, Michaelmas and Christmas sessions for this part of the West Riding were held at Bradford, Leeds and Wakefield. Thus three times a year local men might have visited other centres to respond to indictments for poorly maintained roads, to explain why paupers had not been relieved, to sit on juries, or perhaps to stand trial or give evidence. Each July men from surrounding places would have come to Bradford to attend the Sessions which were usually held at the Moot Hall or at local inns such as the *Sun* or the *King's Arms.* In addition the West Riding treasurer for at least six years in the 1740s was from Bradford, and several local men acted as Chief Bailiffs or were Justices of the Peace.

References in the Quarter Sessions' records to vagrants and peddlers show other types of movement which no doubt brought news of the outside world to Bradford: in 1741 a paster master, or tumbler, who had last performed in Stockport, was apprehended in Bradford; the following year a labourer from Bradford was charged with being idle and disorderly and 'strolling about the county on pretence of selling brandy'; and there were vagrants from such places as Lisburn in Northern Ireland, Perth and Wigan, as well as other parts of Yorkshire.

In addition the church bells were rung on special occasions such as the election of an emperor in 1745, the King of Prussia's victory in 1757 and the taking of Quebec in 1759. The bells were also rung regularly to commemorate the king's birthday, Oak Apple Day, Guy Fawkes Day and other festivals. In 1745, the year of the Young Pretender's uprising, the churchwardens' accounts show that four shillings were paid when 'ye Regiments of Royal Scotts came through ye town'.[10] Some local news would have been spread by the bellman, a postman collected letters from Ferrybridge on the Great North Road and, for those who could read, *The Leeds Mercury* started publication in 1718 and *The Leeds Intelligencer* in 1754.

Until the establishment of the first local Turnpike Trust in 1734, movement would not have been easy for travellers or for goods of any kind. The various processes involved in the growing worsted industry were organised by woolstaplers but carried out by largely independent workers (woolcombers, spinners and weavers) who worked at their homes, some of which were distant from Bradford. The wool, therefore, had to be transported from place to place several times before it was marketed. Coal also was transported by road, and in 1753 it was claimed that Bowling Lane and Little Horton Lane had become almost impassable for wagons and carts, and dangerous for travellers, because of the many heavy carriages, laden with coals, which passed along them.[11] Not everyone welcomed the advent of turnpike roads and the consequent necessity to pay tolls when using them, and there was rioting at Bradford Moor when a new turnpike road was opened there in 1753. The following year three men working on a new road reported the theft of their mattocks (picks) left overnight at a quarry where they were getting stone.[12]

The responsibility for maintaining other local roads was that of the townships, who could be indicted at the Quarter Sessions for failing to keep them in good repair. The township of Bradford was so indicted several times. Each townsman, or a substitute provided by him, was obliged to carry out six days' work on the roads every year, organised by the surveyor, although this work was sometimes commuted into a money payment. The surveyors were unqualified and unpaid, and in 1750 the one for Bowling was accused at the Quarter Sessions that he did:

behave himself negligently and remissly in his duty as to his office belonging and not view the roads, watercourses, bridges, causeways and other ways lying within the said village of Bowling and make presentments of the condition thereof or sufficiently repair the same as he from time to time ought to have done.[13]

The surveyors and other township officers also had to operate under financial constraints. In 1734 an agreement was drawn up by the principal inhabitants of the town of Bradford, in which they make clear their determination to keep control of what was being done, and of what money was being spent in their name. It included an instruction that within two months of leaving office all township officers had to have their accounts examined by two of the principal inhabitants, that any money remaining in the hands of officers had to be passed over to their successors, that no more than six pence per person should be spent on drink at the town's expense when the accounts were handed in, and:

that no surveyor of the highways shall make or amend any new ways, but with the consent and approbation of four or six of the principal inhabitants of the town, except it be by an Order from the Quarter Sessions.[14]

In Manningham a memorandum of May 1760 laid down that no town's officer was to spend more than ten shillings more than his predecessor without giving notice and calling a meeting. If he failed to do this he was to pay the excess sum from his own pocket.[15]

Each township was responsible for maintaining its own poor, and

Figure 4. First workhouse, Barkerend. *Harry Fieldhouse, Old Bradford Illustrated, 1889, p.44.*

appointed overseers of the poor to collect money and distribute it to those in need. The cost of this was rising, and in 1737 and 1738 meetings were held in Bradford to discuss the building of a workhouse for the town 'for the better providing for such people as are or hereafter may be chargeable to the same town.[16] As a result a workhouse was erected in Barkerend at a cost of about £360[17] (Figure 4). The township of Bowling established a workhouse jointly with North Bierley in 1762.[18] The Manningham poor accounts for 1760 show that over half of their money was distributed regularly to an almost constant group of about twenty-four people, while the rest of it was spent on special items such as rent, clothing, doctors' bills and the occasional administrative expense.[19] Those who moved into a township were not necessarily eligible for maintenance; as a result movement was discouraged and there were disputes about people's place of settlement. From disputes dealt with at the Quarter Sessions in the 1740s and 1750s it appears that more families tried to move into Bradford than to leave it.

The agreement made between the principal inhabitants of Bradford in 1734 contained provisions that some of their number should go round the town with the overseers once in every three months to see that no-one had come to settle in the town without a settlement certificate (in which their township of settlement agreed to either receive them back or pay for their support if they should fall on hard times). Those without certificates were to be removed 'by order' to the place of their respective settlements, and no houses in the town were to be let to incomers who could not provide certificates. Similar precautions were being taken in Manningham where in 1760 it was ordered that no Manningham inhabitant should let a cottage to anyone not belonging to the township unless they could provide a certificate.[20]

Constables were appointed to keep order in each township, and the few surviving records show them assisting in the recovery of stolen goods, giving evidence against wrongdoers, escorting prisoners to the House of Correction at Wakefield, and once escorting a prisoner to York Castle.[21] They also helped to collect the county rates, which increased five fold for Bradford, as well as for Bowling, Horton and Manningham, between 1740 and 1760.[22]

The constables were also involved with meetings of the manorial courts, where the upkeep of footpaths, hedges and ditches, the selling of unwholesome food and the use of false weights and measures were among the matters dealt with. Such courts were held about once a month. Other manorial courts met twice yearly when the new owners of houses and land, whether by purchase, inheritance or through marriage, did fealty to the lord of the manor.[23]

In the 1740s and 1750s about thirty Bradford people were prosecuted for theft at the Quarter Sessions. Clothing had often been stolen from shops, or occasionally houses, and there were more substantial commercial thefts such as a pair of worsted combs and 24 lb of combed wool from a workshop, 27 yards of woollen cloth of a blue colour from a warehouse, and 486 lb of wool from a warehouse. Other items stolen included two earthen pots, a parcel of onions, six horseshoes, a cow, ducks and chicken, and several silver pints (pots). Lead and various other building materials were also vulnerable, and masons were often accused of their theft. In 1759 concern about theft led to an agreement by fifty-nine prominent Bradfordians that they would each pay 2s 6d or 3s a year and use this money to prosecute thieves as:

> *several dwelling-houses, shops, warehouses, out-houses, and buildings, within the township of Bradford... have lately been broken open in the night-time, and large quantities of divers sorts of goods, plate, linen, and other things of considerable value been feloniously stolen, taken and carried away, and other great damages done to the inhabitants of the said township.*[24]

As well as surveyors of the highways, overseers of the poor and constables, each township appointed two churchwardens. Their

Figure 5. The parish church. Nineteenth century engraving. *William Scruton's Scrapbook 83, p.112.*

duties were to care for the fabric of the church and churchyard and to see to the running of the services of the church. This included such things as the provision of bread and wine for the communion service, the repair of church windows, the clearing of snow from the churchyard, and the payment of those who rung the church bells. To fulfil these duties they levied an annual rate and kept detailed accounts (Figure 5).

A petition was presented to the Archbishop of York by the vicar and parishioners in 1743 for a faculty to erect a gallery on the south side of the parish church as:

> *the seats and pews in the parish church of Bradford aforesaid already built are not able to contain the number of parishioners that resort to the said parish church to hear Divine Service and Sermons and that for want of room, it is thought several absent themselves.*[25]

This can be taken as an indication that the population of Bradford was increasing, and also shows that the vicar was concerned about the increase of nonconformity in his parish. In the same year he estimated that about a sixth part of the families in the parish were Dissenters: either Presbyterians, Baptists, Methodists or Quakers. Twenty years later this proportion had increased.[26]

Communion services were held on the first Sunday of each month and on major festivals, and in 1743 it was reported that Divine Service was read at the parish church on Sundays, Wednesdays, Fridays and Holy Days, while in 1764 Divine Service was performed every Sunday, and sermons were preached in both the morning and the afternoon.[27]

A Presbyterian meeting-house had been built in the Turles in 1719 to replace an earlier chapel in the locality and by the 1740s meetings were held there every Sunday. In 1743 the Baptists were meeting every Sunday, and ten years later a church was formed, at first meeting in a dwelling-house and then in the former cockpit. In 1755:

> *a new erected building situate at the west end of the town of Bradford ... [was] certified ... to be used as a place of meeting for the religious worship of Protestant Dissenters commonly called Baptists.*[28]

In 1743 the vicar referred to teachers called Methodists 'who sometimes come amongst us, and draw great numbers after them' but was uncertain of the times and places of their meetings. John Wesley preached in Bradford and its vicinity several times in the mid-1740s and as a result a 'class' was formed in Bradford. In 1756 the Methodists began to meet at the cockpit, recently vacated by the

Baptists, and Wesley preached there in 1757.[29] When, a few years later, the floor of this building collapsed, the Methodists met for a few years in a barn belonging to James Garnett of the Paper Hall. The vicar reported in 1764 that the Methodists usually attended the parish church, holding their own services before and after the church services. Two years later the Octagon Chapel in Great Horton was opened and was no doubt attended by the Bradford Methodists. The times of its services were nine in the morning, one in the afternoon and five in the evening, still avoiding a clash with the services at the parish church.[30]

There was a Quaker meeting-house in Goodmansend which had been built in 1737, succeeding one built at the end of the previous century.[31] In 1743 it was reported that the Quakers met on Sundays and Wednesdays. Two years later the dwelling-house of Benjamin Bartlett at Stott Hill, Bradford was also certified at the Quarter Sessions to become a Quaker meeting place.[32]

Bradford Grammar School, situated next to the parish church, had been granted a charter by Charles II in 1662, but the school had already been in existence then for at least a century. The Reverend Benjamin Butler was appointed headmaster in 1728, and Thomas Northrop became usher, or assistant master, in 1737. Greek and Hebrew were taught by the headmaster and Latin by the usher, and lessons started each morning at seven o'clock, not finishing until five o'clock, except on Wednesday and Saturday afternoons, devoted to writing, when they finished at three o'clock.[33] Care was taken to instruct the boys 'in the principles of the Christian religion, according to the doctrine of the Church of England.' By 1743 the number of boys being taught had declined to about sixty, half the number who were being educated there twenty-five years earlier, and by 1764 the numbers had declined still further to about forty. Little is known about other education available in the town, but in 1724 a charity of £10 a year had been left by Thomas Ferrand, a Dissenter, for the teaching of children to read and write English, and in the 1750s a Mrs Betty Ward kept a school at Broadstones where she taught writing and accounts.[34]

This account of Bradford has attempted to portray a community which in some ways was a self-contained and isolated place where everyone knew nearly everyone else, a fact that clearly emerges from the examinations of witnesses before the Justices of the Peace after a crime when few wrongdoers escaped identification. But it was also part of a wider world with improving communications and a growing involvement with the worsted trade.

Figure 6. Bradford and the surrounding area. *Thomas Jefferys, The County of York Survey'd*, 2nd edition, 1775.

Notes and References

1 Pontefract Deanery Inventories 1740-1760. Borthwick Institute of Historical Research, University of York.

2 Information about occupations is from E.M. Willmott, *Bradford 1740-1760: a Yorkshire town and its administration*, unpublished Huddersfield Polytechnic MA Thesis, 1986, and E.M. Willmott, Occupations in eighteenth century Bradford, *Bradford Antiquary*, 3rd.series, No.4, 1989, pp 67-77.

3 William Cudworth, The first Bradford Waterworks, *Bradford Antiquary*, vol.4, 1905, pp 353-359.

4 William Cudworth, The Bradford Soke, *Bradford Antiquary*, vol.1, 1880, pp 74-80.

5 C. Richardson, *A Geography of Bradford*, 1976, pp 2,15.

6 Daniel Defoe, *A tour through the Whole Island of Great Britain*, 1724-6; abridged and edited by Pat Rogers, 1971, p.493.

7 Quarter Sessions Rolls April 1760 (Pontefract). W[est] Y[orkshire] A[rchive] S[ervice]:Wakefield QS.

8 A. Everitt, 'The English Urban Inn 1560-1760', pp 104-120 of A. Everitt,ed. *Perspectives of English urban history*, 1973.

9 Quarter Sessions Rolls July 1741 (Bradford). WYAS:Wakefield QS.

10 Bradford Churchwardens' Accounts. Bradford Cathedral.

11 26 George II c83, quoted in W. Cudworth, *Histories of Bolton and Bowling*, 1891, p 196.

12 Quarter Sessions Rolls October 1754 (Leeds). WYAS:Wakefield QS.

13 Quarter Sessions Indictment Book July 1750. WYAS:Wakefield QS.

14 Bradford Township Book, 1734. Bradford Cathedral 74.

15 Manningham Township Book 1760. WYAS:Bradford 40D77.

16 Document of 19 November 1737. Bradford Cathedral 89.

17 William Scruton, *Pen and pencil pictures of old Bradford*, 1889, p 112.

18 Bowling Township Book 1762. WYAS:Bradford 15D74/10/2/1.

19 Manningham Poor Accounts 1760. WYAS:Bradford 15D74/10/2/2.

20 Manningham Township Book 1760. WYAS:Bradford 40D77.

21 West Riding Treasurer's Accounts 1740-1,1741-2,1756-7. WYAS:Wakefield QD2/2-4.

22 West Riding County Rate Estreats Christmas 1739/40 and Midsummer 1760. WYAS:Wakefield QD2/191 and 232.

23 Bradford Court Baron Verdicts. WYAS:Bradford, Deed Box 8, case 1.

24 Document printed in *Bradford Antiquary*, vol.2, 1895, pp 216-217.

25 Petition 27 November 1743. Bradford Cathedral 114.

26 S.L. Ollard & P.C. Walker, eds. *Archbishop Herring's Visitation Returns 1743*, Yorkshire Archaeological Society Record Series, vol.171, 1928, pp 59-60, and C. Annesley & P. Hoskin, eds. *Archbishop Drummond's Visitation Returns 1764*, 1997, pp 76-77.

27 *Ibid.*

28 Quarter Sessions Order Book 1755. WYAS:Wakefield QS.

29 N.Curnock, ed. *The Journal of the Rev John Wesley...* vol.3, 1912.

30 W.Stamp, *Historical notices of Wesleyan Methodism in Bradford and its vicinity*, 1841, p. 49.

31 H.R. Hodgson, *The Society of Friends in Bradford*, 1926, p 26.

32 Quarter Sessions Order Book 1745. WYAS:Wakefield QS.

33 T.Wright, ed. *Autobiography of Thomas Wright of Birkenshaw ... 1736-1797*, 1864, p. 15.

34 *Ibid.*

3. SCHOOL DAYS (1931-1944)

by Arnold Kellett

THESE MAY NOT HAVE BEEN the happiest days of my life, but they have certainly left me with many pleasurable memories, and, in general, I am immensely grateful for the education I received in the days when Bradford was still the wool capital of the world.

Memory is, of course, selective and I have only the vaguest recollection of my very first school - the Infants at Wibsey - where I started in 1931. I can just picture the busy little headmistress, Miss Poynton, daughter - so my father told me - of the Reverend Joseph Poynton, Congregational minister at Wibsey for thirty years, until he moved to Leyburn in 1913.

Buttershaw (St Paul's) School

After a short time at Wibsey Infants it was the policy to move us to a school at the other side of the village - about as far from my St Enoch's Road home to walk - the Church of England Buttershaw School, next to St Paul's Church. Memories of those years start to come into focus, especially of our class-teacher, Mr Cooper, a friendly man, yet with good, unobtrusive discipline and a love of cricket. He was later appointed headmaster at Buttershaw Junior School, Farfield Avenue. One or two little cameos stand out: the regular sessions of the 'percussion band', for example. How I used to envy the ones who managed to get a turn on the drums, whilst I had to be content with a triangle, castanets or tambourine! In absolute contrast to this tuneless racket was the two minutes silence I remember so well... . We stood there like little statues, at the eleventh hour, on the eleventh day of the eleventh month on what we always called Armistice Day. There was a real atmosphere of solemnity that I can still feel. The sparse traffic in the streets, and even the very dogs and cats, it seemed, obediently stood still for those two long minutes.

In the 1930s, of course, memories of the Great War were still horribly fresh to most of our parents and teachers. In our sitting-room at home was a small glass cabinet displaying the medals won by my father's elder brother, killed at Arras in 1917 at the age of twenty-two. His name was Walter Arnold Kellett... . I have always been aware that I was named after this handsome, promising young

Figure 1. School photograph of the author. *Arnold Kellett*

uncle I never knew, but whose photographs I used to see. So, even as a small schoolboy, I filled my two minutes silence with thoughts of a member of our family who had been blown to bits by a German shell (Figure 1).

A happier national occasion I can just remember was the Silver Jubilee of George V and Queen Mary in 1935, when every schoolchild received a special mug and a generous medallion of chocolate in an embossed tin, which I still treasure.

A May Day Pageant

My sharpest memory of the years at Buttershaw is of a little pageant we presented on May Day 1936, I think. It was a re-enactment of the Bradford Legend, and took place in hot sunshine on Wibsey fairground. By then we all knew why the coat-of-arms featured a Boar's Head - the beast of Cliffe Wood that had terrorised the medieval inhabitants of Bradford. In the pageant I was chosen to play the part of the dishonest fellow who came across the boar, already killed, and cut off its head, falsely claiming the reward as the one who had killed it. To make it authentic they actually gave me a real pig's head to hold - freshly decapitated by a Wibsey butcher. Though it was wrapped in grease-proof paper, I remember how bloody and messy it was as I lugged it around with me - and how it stank in the heat. My pal, Stanley Evans, was luckier. He played the part of the hero who had killed the boar and cut out the tongue to prove it. All he had to carry was a real pig's tongue, also from the butcher's, and I can see and hear him now as he proudly denounced me and claimed the reward. I don't think this early casting in the role of a villain did me any harm - but every time I see that stark and tongueless boar on the Bradford coat-of-arms, the memory of that smelly pig's head comes flooding back.

This pageant alone gives the lie to the notion that in those days education was no more than a dreary round of drumming home the three Rs. Here was history being brought to life - not just any old history, but that of our own city, something with which we could really identify. That early historical re-enactment has been, I think,

Figure 2. May Day pageant, Wibsey, 1936. *Telegraph & Argus.*

the inspiration behind my own dramatised presentations of the history of Knaresborough, including the Millennium Pageant of June 2000.

We had our pictures in the paper following that May Day (Figure 2). There is a happy tableau showing some of the players, including Perry Smith, sitting cross-legged at the front, who had taken the part of the herald, and who in adult life became a Methodist minister, serving mainly in Australia. In the centre of the tableau is the Lady Mayoress of Bradford (Mrs J. Pearson) who is crowning a member of our class as May Queen. She was Dorothy Sutcliffe - and even at that young age I remember thinking how pretty she was.

Dorothy was to impinge on our lives in a very different way when tragedy struck a few years later. Not long after that May Day, however, she was still the star turn in our class as we moved back to Wibsey Modern School - I say 'back', because it was adjacent to the Infants, where we had started. Here we had an intensive one-year preparation for the 'scholarship' exam, forerunner of the 'eleven-plus'.

Wibsey Modern School

We could not have been better prepared for this than by our class-teacher, Miss E.M. Fretwell. Many will remember this formidable lady as the classic old-style schoolmistress, with a no-nonsense sit-up-and-pay-attention routine. I see her now as large, plump, bespectacled, consistently strict, with a manner varying from bleak and snappy (knuckles *were* rapped in those days) to the maternal and almost jolly. Her speech, with its habitual menacing intonation, was rapid, but always clear - and she rarely needed to repeat herself. There was in her lessons no talking out of turn, no answering back - and the slightest hint of silliness was brought to an instant halt with 'Hands on heads!'

It is true that the majority of our teaching consisted of driving home the fundamentals of correct reading, writing and spelling. I see Miss Fretwell now, writing on the blackboard. Occasionally - and unpredictably - she would turn round to peer over her spectacles to check that all heads were assiduously bent to the task - copying the list of spellings she had written up with exemplary neatness, which we had to learn and on which we were always tested. There was a similar emphasis on times tables, of course, chanted away like mantras, but giving us the basis for a life-time of automatic numerical responses.

Yet Wibsey Modern School, as its name suggested, was influenced by new ideas and the pioneering spirit that still characterised education in Bradford in the years before the Second World War. Various colourful things came along to brighten the traditional school day. For example, I vividly recall being summoned to appear before the headmaster, the fearsomely strict but kind-hearted Mr Mann. I had apparently won the Scripture Prize, and I had to choose from a list of books deemed suitable for devout little children. They were mostly edifying titles such as *Pilgrim's Progress*, but I chose - greatly to Mr Mann's amusement - the only one that appeared to have no Christian connection whatever, a cowboy tale called *The Settler of Serpent Creek*.

The Silent Screen

Miss Fretwell herself did much to add relief and variety to our essential scholarship fare. Imagine the excitement of ten and eleven year olds at being asked to take part in the making of a movie, even if it was - unlike the ones we were already allowed to see at the Saturday matinee at the Cosy Cinema - a silent film. To think that in the context of what many think of as the dull world of the 3Rs we had

Figure 3. Miss Fretwell, with Dorothy Sutcliffe (left) and Molly Waterhouse, the author and Geoffrey Burston (cook). *Arnold Kellett.*

Figure 4. The cast of *Elfland Wants a Cook*, 1937, showing the author, finger bandaged, filmed by Mr N.E. Scott. *Telegraph & Argus.*

the chance to be film stars! The film, *Elfland Wants a Cook* was made by the father of a girl in our class, Mr N.E. Scott, one of the 9.5 mm black and white enthusiasts typical of the pre-war years, and a member of the Bradford Cine Circle (Figure 3).

We did the filming in Judy Woods, taking the whole of one sunny day, with Miss Fretwell as director and Mr Scott as cameraman. The story concerned a group of woodland elves who were so dissatisfied with their meals that they decided to kidnap two human girls to do them some decent cooking. The girls were played by Dorothy Sutcliffe, the former May Queen, and her equally charming friend, Molly Waterhouse. I was one of those chosen to be an elf - not just an ordinary elf, but one always into mischief. In one scene I had to sneak up to the two girls, steal a gooseberry from the pile they had ready for a pie they were making, bite into it, and pull a wry face. Then I did a scene in which I picked up a knife from the girls' woodland kitchen, and cut my finger. A photograph later appeared in the *Yorkshire Observer* and also in the *Telegraph and Argus* showing me in the centre of a group of elves, pulling another kind of face as my cut finger was being bandaged up by Molly Waterhouse (Figure 4).

Those two girls must have been exhilarated by their experience of being film stars, especially when the film was shown to a large audience by the Bradford Cine Circle. Years later, I understand, the film was thrown out along with some rubbish. I was glad that Dorothy Sutcliffe, in particular, had her moment of glory. A year or two later, when we were at secondary school, we heard the shocking news that she had died of what was then called 'infantile paralysis' (polio).

Scholarship Days

Standard IVA, as our class was known, was duly entered for the scholarship exam. I can't remember much about the exam itself - only the great day when the results arrived, and Miss Fretwell handed out envelopes telling our parents whether or not we had passed to go to a grammar school. I remember that a number of the envelopes, including mine, had the much-prized 'red tick' on the envelope, indicating that a place was available, assuming fees on a sliding scale were paid. One boy in our class had been specially commended for a high mark in arithmetic. Alas, he was from 'a poor home', and his parents, we were told, could not afford to send him to grammar school. I can see him now. not as well dressed as the rest of us, and his nose always seemed to be running but he had a bright eye, and his hand was always up in arithmetic lessons. All that potential wasted. I have often wondered what happened to him.

The move to Carlton

Our parents had a choice of grammar schools, but there was one reason why it had to be Carlton for me. It was not just because it was conveniently on the southern side of the town, near the Technical College. It was where my father's brother, killed at Arras, had been educated (one of forty-two Carlton boys killed in the war). In his day it would be known as 'Carlton Street', a term used for a long time by older Bradfordians. Its official name, when I went there in 1937, was Carlton High School for Boys. The absence of girls made it a rougher, tougher sort of place from the start - from the very first day when we stuck out like sore thumbs in the playground and, by ancient custom, the older boys kept kicking our embarrassingly brand-new leather schoolbags.

We had bright new uniforms, too; a cap and a royal blue jacket with a blazing torch on the breast pocket, bearing a Latin motto about the light of learning. This three-form entry school of around 450 was divided into four school houses, unimaginatively named after four colours - no doubt by some lack-lustre committee attempting in advance of the times to be politically correct. I was

Figure 5. Dr S.E.J. Best, Head of Carlton, 1935-1944. *The Carltonian, December 1944.*

thankful to be placed in Red House. It could have been Green or Blue - but by a merciful providence it was not Brown! The lads who had the misfortune to be allocated to Brown House were, I'm afraid, the butt of lavatorial jokes throughout their time at school.

Wartime schooldays

In the last two years before the Second World War started there was a full school programme, including a Shakespeare production and orchestral concerts. Drama was one of the luxuries that unfortunately had to go during the war years, but I do not remember much in the way of deprivation. In some ways we were cushioned from the war while we were in school. There was a kind of civilising atmosphere introduced by the headmaster, Dr S.E.J. Best, who had been appointed there (from a school in Gravesend) in 1935 (Figure 5). He had, for example, brightened the school corridors with framed prints, especially of French impressionists. He developed the annexe with gym, showers and Sixth Form classrooms and built up games and sport, though for this we had to travel to Green Lane Baths, Odsal Top and Horsfall Playing Fields. There was also a good scout troop run by Mr H.B. Hodgson. Dr Best encouraged visits to the Civic Theatre and formed a school Civic Society. His lasting memorial, though, was the tastefully appointed library, with its quality oak furniture and ample provision of books and journals, said to be the best school library in the West Riding.

The only real upheaval caused by the war was that for a short period Carlton was evacuated to a school in Wyke. When we returned we found that walls had been built to protect the lowest windows from blast. We were never completely free from the general background of sirens, planes, guns and occasional bombs, to say nothing of all the restriction imposed by the blackout and rationing. It might, of course, be thought that wartime education must have been inferior because many good teachers had joined the armed services. But as far as Carlton was concerned, it seemed to work to our advantage.

Many of our teachers, some of whom might otherwise have retired, were the old guard - really experienced schoolmasters who, generally speaking, gave us a first-rate traditional grammar school education. In addition, there were a few women teachers, notably Miss Doris Bushell, inspirational head of English, an attractive art teacher, Miss Simpson, and - brought by the war - a German refugee lady, Frau Bluhm, who read Goethe to us, I remember, in its beautiful original. Some of the women, notably Miss Harrison and Miss Goodby, helped to organise another wartime bonus, the harvest camps at Branston in Lincolnshire, where as Sixth Formers we picked potatoes alongside melodious Italian prisoners of war. It was at these camps that we came to know our teachers as human beings - S.J. Atkinson, for example, head of physics, whom I later came to know as a Methodist organist. S.J. was to be distinguished from P.R. Atkinson, PE, who became a Lieutenant Commander in the RNVR.

Memorable Masters
In the early years, though, the staff were remote and their discipline strict. One of the most feared, yet respected, was the Senior Master, 'Puffy' Perfect. How did this mild, urbane looking gentleman maintain such cast-iron discipline? It may have been something to do with glimpses of him in the school hall caning boys so hard that he, 'Puffy', was quite out of breath. But mainly it was because, fairly early in breaking in a new class, he would suddenly stop, mid-sentence, and furiously roar out at some boy not apparently paying attention: 'See! If ever I have to speak to you again...' Even stricter, perhaps, was 'Charlie' Hudson OBE, old army man, ram rod back, teaching maths to rows of Madame Tussaud's dummies - though he occasionally permitted us to convulse with laughter when he was in the mood, and was an excellent teacher. 'How do I like my eggs frying?' he would bawl out when we made a mess of quadratic equations. And, well-trained, we would shout back in unison: 'On both sides, sir!'

All our teachers seemed to be characters in those days, as though borrowed from the pages of some Dickens novel. Take stocky little 'Blotch', for example, probably so called because of his fiery complexion - Joe Whittaker, renowned teacher of German, who served Carlton for thirty-six years. Then there was 'Twitch' Taylor, versatile teacher of English, 'Joey' Craven, lively teacher of history, 'Dicky' Boyd, teacher of several subjects but especially chemistry. When we were in the third form 'Dicky', a big, corpulent man, would bellow out insults at us, such as, 'Yer copper-coloured ostrich!'. And one morning he gave us a marvellous demonstration of old-style teaching.

For homework he had told us to learn the long definition which begins, 'The equivalent weight of any element or compound'. The next day he pointed to various lads who had to stand up and recite it. Then he told the whole class to recite it. 'Again!' he shouted - and once more we parroted it off. 'Again!' 'And again!' This went on for most of the lesson. 'And just once more!' (but it never was). Still I guarantee that no boy in our class could ever fail to rattle off that definition till his dying day even on his dying day! Head of chemistry was a more conventional master, a lovely man who always inspired me to come top in his subject, Mr. L. Whalley, who was later also Senior Master and acting Head.

The most entertaining lesson of all was French, certainly when taken by 'John Henry', the name always given to J.H. Hird, who was later well-known as Dr Joseph Hird, author of the delightful *Mirfield: Life in a West Riding Village* (1900-1914). He was also a talented violinist and once brought his family along to play 'Eine kleine Nachtmusik' for the Music Club I had started. Best of all he taught us the French songs I can still sing, in particular, 'La Marseillaise'. Conscientious and systematic teacher though John Henry was, I'm afraid we played him up disgracefully. I can see him now, going round the well-separated, padlocked desks, marking our work - always with his gasmask in its cardboard box, slung over his shoulder on string. Not surprising, really, as we once let off a stinkbomb in his lesson and he had to clear the room. As I was good at French, and eventually ended up teaching it myself, I suppose I tried to look as normal as possible to my classmates, and sometimes joined in when they acted the fool. On one occasion he had us chanting that list of pronouns which ends in 'y' and 'en'. I called this out - a second or two later than the others - in such a way that it sounded like 'Hee-Haw!' John Henry, who normally addressed us in French, broke into English with: 'Forward, the donkey!' He then whipped out the short cane that he always carried round with him like some weapon of defence, tucked up his left sleeve, and in front of the class gave me such a caning on the palm of my left hand that I can still feel the long-lasting sting of it.

The Sixth Form Finale

We fooled around in other ways, too, especially when we had the comparative freedom of being in the Sixth Form, mainly in the annexe. In one memorable 'private study' period we were dropping little bombs out of a high window (made from chemicals pinched from the laboratory.) so they exploded in the yard below - not too noticeable, as the yard was outside the noisy metalwork department. I remember seeing Bert Crewe pick up the paper containing the pile of explosive powder - and there was a blinding flash. We staggered out of the fume-filled room, followed by Bert - minus eyebrows, wearing only half a tie, and with a burnt-away shirt and scorched stomach. Mr Templeman, the young Welshman in charge of PE, who also taught geography and was a fine pianist, happened to catch us cleaning him up. He did not, thank God, report us to the Head. If he had, Bert might not have gone on to become Professor Albert Alexander Crewe of Chicago - the first man to photograph the atom.

Figure 6. Cover of *The Carltonian*, designed by Mr L. Evans, Head of Art. *Arnold Kellett.*

Bert, with other Sixth Formers who took science at A Level, was not called up into the armed forces. I was. My father had gone to see the Head in 1942, pointing out that if I did languages in the Sixth I would not be reserved. 'Oh,' said Dr Best. 'If the war goes on that long, we'll all be carrying guns!' Rich, coming from him, who was a Quaker! On the day I was called up into the army my father said, 'Next time you see Best, lad, ask 'im where 'is gun is!'

In 1942, when the war was at its height, I had taken my School Certificate exam, and passed in all nine subjects, seven with an A grade. I went on to make the most of my time in the Sixth, where I was exalted to the rank of Prefect and Bell Boy, with the vital routine, strange to one so unpunctual, of ringing a handbell at strategic points throughout the school to mark the lesson-changes. English lessons with Norman Furlong were a joy - and my interest in writing was further encouraged when Miss Bushell appointed me editor of the school magazine, *The Carltonian* (Figure 6). The issue for 1944 marked the end of an era. Not only was it my swan-song, but it paid tribute to Dr Best, who left at the same time to become Head of Doncaster Grammar School. I tried to put into verse my indebtedness to the school that had opened up so many promising avenues for me and my friends. It was a parody of Gray's *Elegy* and opened:

> *Where each drab mill a sullen chimney rears*
> *To vomit its eternal sooty palls,*
> *When I could boast of but eleven years,*
> *I first surveyed old Carlton's sombre walls.*

Yes. That was the Bradford of smoke-blackened buildings, with mill-chimneys bristling all round us as we went on the roller-coaster tramride down St Enoch's Road into town. Not the most promising of educational backgrounds. Yet I am sure that many others can look back in gratitude to the foundation they received in Bradford schools - not just Carlton, but Grange, Belle Vue, Hanson, Thornton, St Bede's, Bolling, St Joseph's and the Boys' and Girls' Bradford Grammar Schools. And if there was one thing we learnt above all else, it was the wisdom of the motto that originally went with the old Boar's Head, 'Labor Omnia Vincit' ('Work conquers everything') - just another way of saying what was so often written on our school reports - 'Must work harder'.

Figure 7. The City of Bradford Coat of Arms (1907-1974). Note the boar's head. *Bradford Libraries.*

Acknowledgment

I am grateful to my friend, Stanley Evans, for confirmation of many of the details in this chapter. He agrees with me that Carlton gave us a top quality education - and his career in agriculture certainly did not suffer from the fact that he was in Brown House!

4. METHODISM IN BRADFORD

by Simon Valentine

FOLLOWING HIS FAMOUS RELIGIOUS EXPERIENCE at Aldersgate Street on 24 May 1738, when he felt his 'heart strangely warmed' and that he 'did trust in God alone for his salvation', John Wesley began a lifetime of preaching which contributed to the revival of religion that arose in eighteenth century Britain, and led to the formation of a new Protestant movement known as Methodism.

Wesley first visited the town of Bradford in May 1744, preaching at Little Horton Hall and a cottage at Sticker Lane.[1] His brother Charles, aptly called the 'sweet singer of Methodism' due to the fact that he wrote over 6,000 hymns (many of which are still sung by Methodists today), visited the town two years earlier while on his way to Newcastle.[2] However, as with the commencement of the Methodist Church in other localities, John Wesley was not the founder of Bradford Methodism: he reaped where others had sown.

One of the earliest pioneers of Methodism in Bradford was the stonemason preacher, John Nelson (Figure 1). Following his conversion in London and return to his native Yorkshire in 1741, Nelson, for about two or three years, worked as an evangelist with the Moravians until, on studying the Bible, he concluded that the

Figure 1. John Nelson, Charles and John Wesley. *Journal of John Nelson, Kendrew, York, 1802* and *J. Pudney, John Wesley and his World, 1978.*

Figure 2. Exterior of the dungeon, Ivegate. *W.W. Stamp, Historical Notices of Wesleyan Methodism in Bradford and its Vicinity, Mason, 1841.*

Brethren were 'fallen people' and 'boars from the German wood'.[3] 'Hewing stone in the day time, and preaching every night' Nelson began to hold cottage meetings in his home at Birstall and travelled throughout the West Riding, including Bradford, preaching wherever he could.

The story of Nelson's imprisonment at Bradford is well-known. In May 1744, the earnest preacher states in his journal how he was arrested by Reverend Coleby, vicar of Birstall, and finding that 'no bail was to be taken for a Methodist (so called)' was impressed as a soldier. He was taken to Bradford and placed in the dungeon situated near the top of Ivegate (Figure 2).

> *When I came into the dungeon, that stunk worse than a hog-sty, by reason of the blood and filth which sink from the butchers who kill over it', 'my soul was so filled with the love of God, that it was a paradise to me'* wrote Nelson.

While imprisoned at Bradford a prayer meeting was held at the dungeon door by a group of local Methodists. 'About ten' that night, states Nelson,

> *several of the people came to the dungeon door and brought me some*

candles, and put me some meat and water in through the hole of the door. When I had eaten and drank I gave God thanks; and we sang hymns almost all night, they without and I within.

Nelson informs us how 'a man who lives in Bradford... though he was an enemy to the Methodists, upon discovering the ill savour of the place' offered ten pounds as bail and himself as prisoner for Nelson's release, but all to no avail. Nelson had to wait until July of that year before he managed to gain a discharge.[4]

According to tradition this person who willingly offered to take Nelson's place was James Eastwood, a local innkeeper. The group that prayed so fervently at the prison door included Betty Firth of Great Horton, a woman who later became an important instrument of introducing Methodism at Wibsey Moor, where she moved to in 1745, living as housekeeper to her uncle, Matthew Sugden. Though not a Methodist, Sugden, at the request of Betty, allowed Nelson to preach in his house every other week, and on at least one occasion, John Wesley. Sugden's house was owned by Edward Leeds, a local magistrate, who on hearing of his tenant's deviancy, threatened to evict him. Sugden blamed his niece, but requested the landlord to hear the preacher for himself. He did so and although 'in no respect whatever a religious man', Leeds 'was so pleased with what he saw and heard, as to befriend the mason-preacher ever after'.[5]

Other early preachers to the Bradford area included John Bennet who, following his union with Methodism in 1743, regularly visited the West Riding. It would appear that Bennet started a society at Heaton as early as 1744 and frequently preached in the house of George and Mary Rendars in Bradford.[6] In his diary Bennet mentions visits to Bradford, Little Horton, Manningham, Shelf and Great Horton. By 1747 Bennet's preaching activities had extended to 'Balden' [Baildon] where he began the first Methodist group and Pudsey.

William Grimshaw, the perpetual curate of Haworth, and his assistants (the so-called 'Grimshaw's Men'), such as Jonathan Maskew, Thomas Colbeck, Thomas Mitchell, Paul Greenwood and others, preached occasionally in Bradford and the surrounding villages warning all who would listen to 'save their souls' and to 'flee from the wrath to come'. According to local tradition Grimshaw, not being allowed to preach in the parish church, spoke at various locations in the open air, 'his particular arena being a spot afterwards occupied as a coal-staith in Well Street'.[7]

William Darney, despite his 'oddities, waywardness, and erratic doctrinal tendencies', had undertaken considerable itinerant labours in the northern counties, preaching at Bradford and Manningham in 1744. Due to the unconventional hymns he regularly composed, and his desire to publish the same, Darney had been told by the Conference of 1751 that

> *unless William Darney would abstain from railing, begging, and printing nonsense, he should not be allowed to preach in any of the Methodist societies and preaching houses.*

In a curious piece of doggerel entitled, *Progress of the Gospel in diverse places in Great Britain*, Darney condemned the town as immoral and decadent, proclaiming:

> *On Bradford likewise, look Thou down,*
> *Where Satan keeps his seat;*
> *Come by Thy power; Lord! him dethrone,*
> *For Thou art very great.*
> *In Windhill, and in Baildon Town,*
> *Thy children simple be;*
> *In Yeadon, and in Menston-Green,*
> *Some truly mourn for thee.*
> *In Ecclesall they're stiff and proud,*
> *And few that dwell therein,*
> *Do shew they've any fear of God,*
> *Or hatred unto sin . . .*

With alacrity the Scottish pedlar wrote:

> *At Bradford dale and Thornton town,*
> *And places all around;*
> *And at Lingbob sometimes at Noon,*
> *The gospel trump we sound.*

One of the earliest Methodist preachers in the area of Harden and Thornton, was Thomas Lee. Born at Keighley in 1727 Lee worked in woollen manufacture until, experiencing a dramatic conversion typical of the revival converts, he became a Wesleyan preacher in 1748. Similarly to John Nelson, Lee worked at his own trade at his home during the day and preached at various locations at night. Mainly due to his efforts Methodist groups were established in the area of Harden Moor, Lingbob and Thornton. Lee later settled at Long Addingham and became the acknowledged 'apostle of Wesleyan Methodism in Wharfedale and Nidderdale', dying in 1786.

Nathaniel Dracup was a significant figure in the origins of

Methodism in Great Horton. Born near Idle in 1729, but moving to Great Horton, he worked as a shuttle-maker and, following a conversion experience under the preaching of John Wesley, he became a preacher establishing a religious society in his own home. This society, typifying the early Methodists who first met for worship in barns, cellars, garrets and even the open air, later built a chapel at Todley in 1766. Although Robert Raikes is traditionally accepted as being the founder of Sunday Schools, Dracup has a reasonable claim to this honour, holding a Sabbath School for children, in Great Horton in 1766, fourteen years before Raikes.

In 1749 a group of Methodist converts began to meet for worship at a farm house called 'the Oaks', the home of John Pickard, at Allerton. Members included James and Isaac Duckworth, Sarah Duckworth, Mary Haigh, and John and Mary Clayton of Daisy Hill, all converts of William Grimshaw. The Claytons were parents of Isaac Clayton, 'a good mathematician and astronomer' who for thirty years was an itinerant preacher, dying at Bradford in 1833.

Bradford became a regular stopping-place for Wesley while on his frequent northern tours. We read in his journal how on 25 April 1745 he preached at Little Horton and then in Bradford, where he laments: 'I could not but observe how God has made void all their labour "who make void the law through faith"'. It was a matter of great disappointment to him how 'out of their large societies in these towns, how small a remnant is left! In Horton, scarce ten persons out of four-score; in Bradford, not one soul'. Wesley experienced trouble at other societies. On a visit to the Eccleshill group in 1776 Wesley wrote in his journal how 'he might as well as have talked to a lot of posts such were their nature'.

Thomas Mitchell in his autobiography recalls how, in about 1746, 'Mr John Wesley came to Bradforth' and 'joined several of us together in a Class, which met about a mile from the town'. However, as Mitchell states: 'But all of them fell back and left me alone; yet afterwards some of them returned'. Wesley, probably referring to the occasion mentioned by Mitchell, states how, after facing a mob at Leeds, and visiting Skircoat Green near Halifax, on 24 February 1746 he 'preached to a quiet congregation at Bradford'.

The visits made by Nelson and the other early preachers to Bradford had apparently made a significant impression on the people of the town for Benjamin Kennet, the local vicar, in his answers to the questions of enquiry made by Archbishop Herring, complained: 'There is also Teachers called Methodists, who sometimes come amongst us, and draw great numbers after them, but the times and places of their Meeting are uncertain'.[8]

As in many other places in England the ugly head of persecution soon rose up against the Methodists in the Bradford area. Bennet informs us how at Yeadon in 1749 the opposition was so fierce that 'the Brethren... could not assemble themselves together in public or private without hazarding their lives'. Three years earlier Thomas Mitchell described how:

> *One evening, while William Darney was*
> *preaching, the Curate of Guiseley came*
> *at the head of a large mob, who threw*
> *eggs in his face, pulled him down, dragged*
> *him out of his house on the ground, and*
> *stamped upon him. The Curate himself then*
> *thought it was enough, and bade them let*
> *him alone and go their way. Sometime after*
> *Jonathan Maskew came. As soon as he began*
> *to speak, the same mob, pulled him down,*
> *and dragged him out of the house. They*
> *then tore off his clothes, and dragged*
> *him along upon his naked back, over*
> *gravel and pavement. When they thought*
> *they had sufficiently bruised him, they*
> *let him go, and went away. With much*
> *difficulty he crept to a friend's house,*
> *where they dressed his wounds and got*
> *him some clothes.*

Mitchell himself was soon to face the fury of the same mob for as he remarks:

> *It was my turn to go next. No sooner*
> *was I at the town, then the mob came,*
> *like so many roaring lions. My friends*
> *advised me not to preach that night;*
> *and undertook to carry me out of*
> *the town. But the mob followed me in a*
> *great rage, and stoned me for near two*
> *miles, so that it was several weeks*
> *before I got well of the bruises I*
> *then received.*[9]

Although the treatment given by the mob to Darney, Maskew and Mitchell was without doubt severe, the Methodists of Bradford remained relatively unscathed by the mob partly because of the inability, or reluctance, of the local clergyman to act. On one occasion, Benjamin Kennet complained to the Archbishop of York about the irregular preaching practices of the early Methodists expressing a wish for measures to be taken to put them down. The Archbishop however replied: 'Oh, let those mad fellows alone', thus preventing the frustrated clergyman from gaining official support for appropriate sanctions.

On his tour of the north in May 1755 Wesley could state with satisfaction how Bradford was 'now as quiet as Birstall'. 'Such a change', remarked Wesley, 'has God wrought in the hearts of the people since John Nelson was in the dungeon here'. In the following year, the second floor of a large building in 'Turles Green' was taken by the Methodist society. This building, known locally as the 'Cock-pit' (Figure 3), had been the original meeting place of the Baptists and later served as a gathering place for the followers of Joanna Southcott, Baron Swedenborg, Prophet Wroe and other sectarian groups. It had also been used as a soldiers' barracks, a court-house, a vagrants' refuge, a soap and oil warehouse and, as the name implied, a place for cock fighting. A local poet, writing about the Methodists' use of the Cockpit, composed the following lines which appeared in the *Gentleman's Magazine* 1798:

> *O, wondrous pile, who can thy use relate?*
> *At once to God and mammon consecrate!*
> *Here Christ is preached, and saving*
> *faith is taught,*
> *Here goods are sold, and merchandise*
> *is bought.*
> *Strange union! So the Temple once was made*
> *The house of praying, and the house of trade*
> *- The Synagogue of Satan!*

On 15 May 1757 Wesley states how he stood on the steps leading up to the Cock-pit and preached to the crowd which had gathered on 'the plain adjoining it' exhorting his hearers to 'follow after Charity'. This building served as a meeting place for the Methodists until the floor eventually gave way. James Garnett, a piecemaker, residing at the Paper Hall, offered the temporary use of his barn at

Figure 3. The Cock-pit. *Evans & Dunwell, Eastbrook Chapel, 1825.*

Figure 4. The Octagon Chapel, Great Horton. *J. Norton Dickons, Kirkgate Chapel, Bradford, 1903.*

Barkerend until a new chapel, octagonal in design, was built on Horton Road in 1766. Wesley, in his journal, states how this new chapel was 'fifty-four feet square, the largest octagon in England'. However, the Octagon also became inadequate due to structural instability, and it was closed in 1810 (Figure 4).

In 1811 the Kirkgate Chapel was opened. This solid, practical, imposing building, with its flight of steps leading to a double fronted facade, cost £9,000 and could seat 1,400 people. The interior, typical of other Nonconformist tabernacles, had varnished wooden pews, the upper gallery and lower floor looking down on a high rostrum of a pulpit with a cathedral like organ behind.[10] (Figure 5).

The old Eastbrook Chapel (Figures 6, 7 and 8), built 'east of the brook' in 1825, was acclaimed for many years as one of the 'handsomest buildings in Bradford'. This, like Kirkgate, was an impressive building seating 1,500 people. Although the famous Dr Adam Clarke, speaking at the opening ceremony, stated that the chapel was 'too far out of the town', the church attracted large congregations and thrived so much that, in 1856, Reverend Thomas

Figure 5. The Kirkgate Chapel. *J. Norton Dickons, Kirkgate Chapel, Bradford, 1903.*

Figure 6. Eastbrook Chapel. *J. Norton Dickins, Kirkgate Chapel, Bradford, 1903.*

Figure 7. The Eastbrook Brotherhood. *Wesleyan Methodist Magazine, 1914.*

Figure 8. Eastbrook Hall as it looks today. *Photograph by S.R.Valentine.*

Vasey could write how at Eastbrook:

> *We are doing pretty well here both*
> *spiritually and financially. As to the*
> *former we have had about 200 conversions*
> *last quarter; and as to the latter we*
> *are raising £4,000 against the debt of*
> *£6,000 and have already secured £2,500.*[11]

Bradford had become a circuit in its own right in 1769. In 1835, indicative of growing congregations and chapel building, the Bradford Circuit was divided into two circuits: Bradford West, with Kirkgate as the main church, and Bradford East, centred at Eastbrook. The West Circuit in that year boasted 1,827 members and eleven churches while the East Circuit had 1,266 members and seven churches.

The national Religious Census of 1851 revealed that the Wesleyan Methodists with twelve Chapels and 9,785 attenders, had as many places of worship as the Established Church, and was the largest Nonconformist body in Bradford. Other Methodist organisations: the Primitive Methodists, the Wesleyan Association and the Methodist New Connexion had a further twelve chapels. This compared favourably with the other denominations: the

Congregationalists had six chapels; the Baptists five while other Nonconformist groups such as the Quakers and Moravians had one chapel each.

The religious survey carried out by the *Bradford Observer* in 1881 revealed that, although, out of a population of over 194,000 only 27.1 per cent attended a place of worship, the Methodists were still retaining their position as the largest Nonconformist organisation, increasing the number of their chapels to twenty-three and attendance had risen to 12,706. The Wesleyan Conference, meeting in Bradford in 1878, gave tangible evidence of the circuit's importance within the Methodist fold.

During the Victorian period the Methodists, like other Nonconformists, becoming more successful (and more respectable) began to build churches on a grand scale throughout the town. The religion of barns and cellars had gone: the age of cathedrals and tabernacles had commenced. With much denominational pride, and often with much denominational flag-waving and trumpet blowing, chapels were built in a style which equalled, and challenged, the splendour of the local parish churches.

White Abbey Chapel, the first Methodist chapel in Manningham, was built in 1838. In the 1850s James Ambler, a local manufacturer, purchased a plot of land and gave it to the local Methodist society, and a further contribution led to the opening of a church on Carlisle Road in 1857. In 1879, St John's, the Cathedral of Bradford Methodism was opened for worship (Figure 9). Built in neo-gothic style with an impressive tower and steeple, St John's was designed to seat 1,000 persons and cost £14,634. It was the only Methodist church in the town which had a regular liturgical service involving a surpliced choir of men and boys.

The new chapel at Allerton, designed by Herbert Issitt and built in 1886, typified the Victorian belief in respectability, permanence and denominational triumphalism. The front facade had an open portico

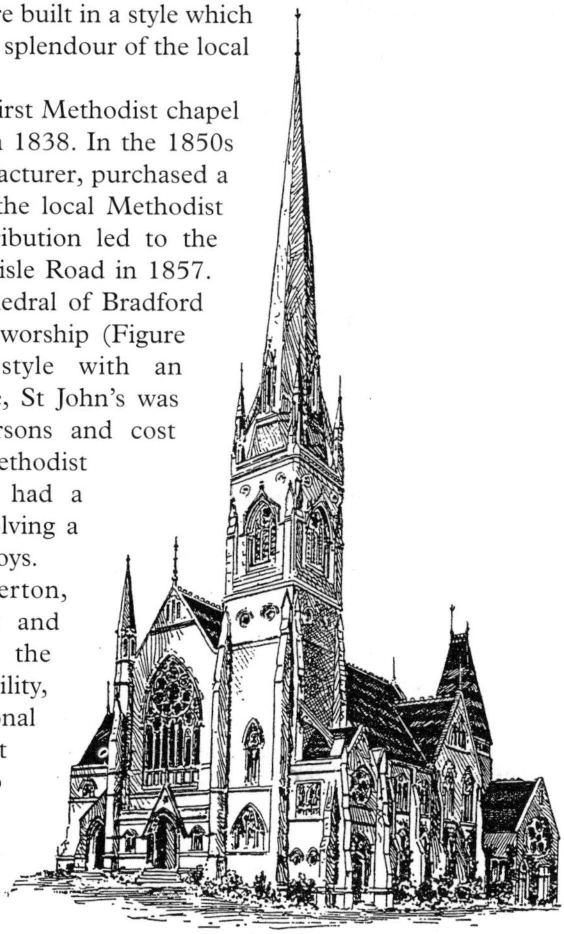

Figure 9. St John's Wesleyan Methodist Church. *W. Cudworth, History of Manningham, Heaton and Allerton, 1896.*

constructed in the Doric style, a large three-light gable window and moulded pediment. Both the front elevation and the side wings were entirely of cleansed Ashlar stone. This building, capable of seating 680 worshippers, was a 'statement' rather than a practical building, bearing witness to an unjustified expectation of larger congregations rather than reflecting the dwindling numbers that regularly assembled within its walls.

The Methodists of Bradford have included the names of some famous, if not fascinating, characters. Benjamin Clough, born in the town in 1791, attended the Kirkgate Chapel and served from 1814 as a missionary in Ceylon [now Sri Lanka] becoming famous for his Singhalese dictionaries, still in use today. Other notable Bradford Methodists have included William Wood Stamp, minister and historian, well-known for his *History of Methodism in Bradford* (1841). He was elected president of the Methodist Conference in 1860. Charles Federer, the Swiss antiquarian, scholar and bibliophile, who made Bradford his home town from 1857, attended the White Abbey Church. Federer's extensive collection of Yorkshire literature now forms an important collection in the city's central library. Henry Mitchell, local stuff merchant and businessman and Mayor of Bradford from 1874 to 1875, was 'a devoted Wesleyan', and the main contributor behind the building of St John's Methodist Chapel.

An excellent example of what can be achieved by one with the right attitude, application and a goodly measure of 'Yorkshire grit' is seen in the life of Joseph Wright. As a child he attended the Sunday School at Bethel Primitive Methodist Chapel at Windhill, Shipley. At the age of six he worked in the local quarries caring for the donkeys, at seven gained employment at nearby Salt's Mill and at thirteen worked as a sorter. While weaving he taught himself to read and write and gained a post as a teacher. He continued to study and, by sheer determination and effort, was appointed Professor of Comparative Philology at Oxford in 1891.

A man of eccentricity, yet rock-like reliability and honesty, was James Boocock,: grocer and warp dresser. When working in his shop he kept his Bible under the counter ready to provide encouragement when tempted or to find a 'word in season' which might lead to the conversion of any unsuspecting person who entered his business premises. Boocock had no bell on his door. Instead he trained a parrot, at the appearance of a customer, to call out: 'Shop Boocock, shop Boocock'. He was an enthusiastic Methodist from the age of fourteen to his death seventy-two years later in 1895, serving in that time as both teacher and superintendent of the Sunday School,

Chapel Steward and local preacher in the Shipley Circuit.

Although, as the Secretary of the 1887 Conference remarked, 'Methodism in Yorkshire is in a state of inexorable decline', there were still several centres of considerable Methodist influence at that time throughout the county and particularly so in Bradford. Due to the work of Hugh Price Hughes and the Forward Movement, central Mission Halls appeared in towns and cities all over Britain. In 1904 Eastbrook Hall was opened with its aim to 'reach and win the unchurched masses', catering for both the physical and the spiritual needs of the urban poor. Built on the site of the old Eastbrook Chapel the Hall, designed by Messrs W.J. Morley & Sons of Bradford, was octagonal in shape, accommodating 2,000 people and cost £23,000.

The Reverend H.M. Nield, superintendent of the Hall, was a pioneer in presenting a message relevant to the working man. He would hold debates and lectures which were widely advertised and well attended. One such was on gambling which he named 'what'll Win', the slogan used in a leading racing paper. In the week prior to the address he received a postcard with the name of the likely winner at a forthcoming race meeting. During his address he read out the postcard, and the horse named won the race. The following week saw many more interested men arrive at the meeting!

A popular event at Eastbrook Hall was the Brotherhood where, even as late as 1914, on a Sunday afternoon 3,000 men regularly met together. In 1905 the Sisterhood was formed with as many as 2,000 women attending. The women's meeting, formed in an attempt not only to 'save' the working-class mother, but also to rescue 'fallen women', had over 700 members. Similarly the Sunday School had over 900 children attending weekly. The Gospel Chariot, an open-air pulpit on wheels, drawn by horses, was used to great effect throughout the town by Nield and his assistant evangelists keen to invite all to attend the meetings.[12]

The influence for good brought about by Eastbrook Hall is clearly seen in the following anecdote. A reliable source told how a businessman was interviewing a woman at a house in the city centre. During that conversation the woman said to the man: 'I say, what do you think of my little home?' 'It does you credit, Missus', the man replied, 'everything is so very nice indeed'. Much to his surprise the woman continued by saying:

Its Eastbrook Hall that's done it! My husband used to give me a few shillings a week, and me and the children were half starved and half clothed. Our furniture was then mainly orange box furniture. Then he went to Eastbrook Brotherhood. Now he brings home his money instead of spending it on drink. Now we are as well-fed and well clothed as anyone else in our position, and instead of orange box furniture we have got this nice little home together. I thank God that Eastbrook Hall was ever built.[13]

In 1901 there were forty-two Wesleyan Methodist Chapels in Bradford with many other chapels belonging to the other strands of Methodism such as the Primitive Methodists, the Methodist New Connexion and the Wesleyan Reformers. However, this was the peak of Methodist growth in Bradford. In the postwar period Methodism, like most other religious organisations in the city, began to decline. Eastbrook Hall was closed in the mid-1980s, and partially destroyed by fire in 1996. Many churches have closed and been demolished or are now used as warehouses and shops. But yet the Methodists of Bradford still have a significant place in the life of the city. Their social concern, as well as their evangelistic fervour, are seen in the work carried out by various city centre projects and of course in the activities of each of the local churches.

Notes and References

1 N. Curnock, *Journal of John Wesley*, Standard Edition, 1938, 17 May 1744.

2 T. Jackson, *The Life of Charles Wesley*, Mason, London, 1841, vol 2, p. 117.

3 *Journal of John Nelson*, Kendrew, York, 1804, p. 53.

4 S.R. Valentine, 'Significant Inroads into satan's seat, Early Methodism in Bradford 1740-1760,' *Proceedings of the Wesley Historical Society*, May 1998, pp. 141-155.

5 W.W. Stamp, *Historical Sketches of Wesleyan Methodism in Bradford and its Vicinity*, Mason, 1841.

6 S.R. Valentine, *John Bennet and the Origins of Methodism and the Evangelical Revival in England*, Scarecrow, NJ, 1998.

7 Stamp, *op cit*, p. 16.

8 S.L. Ollard & P.C. Walker, eds, *Archbishop Herring's Visitation Returns*, 1743, Yorkshire Archaeological Society, 5 vols, Wakefield, 1928-1933.

9 T.Mitchell, *Memoirs of Thomas Mitchell*, 1746.

10 J. Norton Dickons, *Kirkgate Chapel, Bradford, and its Association with Methodism*, 1903.

11 T.Vasey, *The Memoirs of Thomas Vasey*, Bradford, 1864.

12 L.A.J. Heywood, *The Story of a Great Achievement, 50 Glorious Years: A History of Eastbrook Hall*, 1954 and Wesleyan Methodist Magazine, 1914, pp. 447f.

13 Heywood, *op cit.*

5. FULL CIRCLE AT ILKLEY: HYDROTHERAPY TO HOUSECRAFT

by Pat Brown

CHARLES DARWIN COMPLETED the *Origin of Species* in 1859 and spent the next two months recovering his health at a large hydropathic hotel in Ilkley. The establishment, built in 1853 on the edge of Ilkley Moor high above the town of Ilkley, was called Wells House. The land was bought from Peter Middleton, the local squire, by a joint stock company. The directors employed Cuthbert Broderick, the architect of Leeds Town Hall, and the extensive gardens were landscaped by Joshua Major, well-known for his earlier work on the Manchester parks. The work on the building was completed and the hydropathic hotel opened for business on 28 May 1856, at a cost of around £30,000 (Figure 1).

Ilkley, owed some of its earlier growth to the nineteenth century medical belief that certain springs and wells had healing properties. White Wells was the site of the original spring and is to be found on the moor directly across from Wells House. As early as 1706 poor people in the town used to receive treatment there funded from

Figure 1. Wells House at the time of the Grand Opening in 1856. *Bradford College*

money raised by public subscription. However, the real growth of the town began with the arrival of the railway system. Prior to this, horse-drawn carriages would travel to Arthington - the railway system's furthest extension from Leeds - and transport visitors to the town. The hotel had its own stables complete with carriages and horses. In 1865 the Midland and Eastern Railway Company extended the lines from Leeds to Ilkley - one through Guiseley and the other through Otley. A timetable of 1868 shows that a traveller could leave Ilkley at 7.45am and arrive in London at 3.15pm!

Visitors would travel large distances to 'take the cure' at Wells House which had a resident medical practitioner. An early prospectus gives a detailed insight into the organisation of the establishment. Medical direction was provided by Dr Scott whose apparent 'extended experience and reputation as a hydropathic and general practitioner afford sufficient guarantee for careful and judicious treatment.'[1] The treatment advocated at the time combined hydropathy with pure air and a well regulated and varied diet. Too violent or injudicious application of the water stimulus was considered extremely dangerous to persons of a 'delicate habit'. Wells House possessed a large variety of baths:- Turkish, Compressed Air, Electro-Chemical, Ascending and Descending Douches, Rain or Needle, Rose Spray, Shower, Russian Vapour, Lamps, Running Sitz, Hot and Cold, and Medicated Baths of every description. It was discreetly noted that there were separate baths for ladies and gentlemen.

The building boasted a sheltered promenade one hundred yards in length, a Winter Garden and spacious rooms which were heated in winter by 'Sylvester's warm air apparatus'. Recreation took the form of American bowling alleys, tennis courts, croquet lawns, and a winter ice-skating rink. The more adventurous guests could perhaps be tempted onto the 'open and breezy moorlands'.

The tariff for the hotel makes fascinating reading. Rooms were charged on a weekly basis dependent on the floor level and available views. A first floor room between Easter and the end of June cost £3 13s 6d (£3 67.5p) per week, 12s 6d (62.5p) per day, whilst the same room from July to the end of September rose to £4 4s 0d (£4.20p). Food and treatments were charged in addition to this but if visitors shared a double bed a reduction of 5s (25p) per week was made! Breakfast cost 2s 6d (12.5p), whilst dinner cost a shilling (5p) more. There is no mention of lunch, perhaps it interfered with the treatment schedules. Room sevice was available but carried its own special charges. Servants accompanying visitors had to use servants' quarters or were charged a guinea per week extra. Other charges were made by the doctor who required 10s 6d (52.5p) for the introductory consultation fee and a weekly charge of the same amount for his attendance. The range of bathing treatments had the following charges:-

Tickets for a series of six baths were 12s 0d (62p)

Turkish, Medicated, Electric or Compressed Air 1s 6d (5.5p)

Electricity or rubbing, in any form, per day 1s 0d (5p)

Douche, Needle, Shallow, Sitz, Plunge or Warm, each 1s 0d (5p) or 5s 0d (25p) per week.

Blankets and sheets for bathing could be purchased from the House or visitors could bring their own.

Bath attendants were on duty for three two hour shifts starting at 6.30am each day but the baths closed at 10.00am on Sundays. Prayers took place in the drawing room on Sunday evenings at 9.30pm. As guests were recommended to retire early, strict quiet had to be maintained in the establishment after 10.00pm. There was a full complement of servants to see to the needs of the wealthy guests, including a wine waiter and head waiter. Guests bringing their own wine were charged 2s (10p) per bottle corkage. It was in this environment that Charles Darwin stayed for two months in 1859. His wife, servants and children rented a house on Wells Road, a short distance away, to be near him whilst he recovered from the exhaustion attached to writing his famous book.

From Hotel to College

Medical opinion gradually changed regarding hydropathic treatments. They were linked to various scandals of the times and *The Lancet* refused to enter into any discussion on the subject. Various people had been permanently maimed and injured by the indiscriminate use of baths and the fortunes of the hydros began to decline. The emphasis was placed on the holiday aspect rather than on taking 'the cure' and visitors tended to stay at the hotel as a healthy alternative to the fast growing industrial towns. Indeed many wealthy industrialists from Leeds and Bradford built their homes in Ilkley after experiencing its restorative powers. Wells House remained a hotel until the Second World War when its surprised guests were given just twenty-four hours to leave the building, when it became the offices and nerve centre of the Wool Control. This body was responsible for the supply and production of all the woollen uniforms needed for our armed forces during the period of the war. At the end of the war the building was vacated and had several short-term uses before it was purchased by the West Riding County Council in1950 at a cost of £40,000. Major building work followed to enable the building to accommodate the first of some forty housecraft students at the newly designated College of Housecraft. Refurbishment accounted for £148,000. Miss Glen was the Principal and it was to take a further three years before the college was officially opened in 1954 at a final cost of £250,000. There were now some 150 students, fourteen lecturers and six administrative staff.

At the official opening Lady Ogilvie, Principal of St Anne's College, Oxford, declared 'what the West Riding thought in education today, the rest of the country thought tomorrow.' Ilkley College of Housecraft was seen to be a flagship of its time believing that a good home was the basis of a good life and that the students had a mission to fulfil in training the housewives and mothers of the future. Housecraft was perceived as something more than just domestic science and for those who taught it 'would imbue pupils with a desire for taste, dignity and originality in the furnishing and decoration of the home'.[2]

In 1963 I applied to Ilkley College of Housecraft to train as a teacher and arrived one September afternoon for interview. The three-year course started in the following January and was unusual in two respects - one, that it was of three years' duration, when general courses had only been two years, and secondly that it began in January rather than September as most other colleges did. I arrived along with my examination certificates, in best clothes, including a straw boater, and was invited to write a discourse on my choice of college and venue. The moors and magnificent rugged scenery played no small part in my scribblings as did the wonderful building, the like of which I had never experienced before (coming as I did from a terraced house in a northern industrial cotton town). I thought I was aiming for the moon and had about as much chance of getting there. Two days later I was offered a place.

My father took the morning off work to drive me to college through the snow and ice. The thirty-mile journey was fraught with hazards and took several hours. The moor looked very inhospitable as we climbed the final few hundred yards to the large solid doors at the front of the building. He placed my suitcase on the doorstep and drove straight off - not being one to prolong farewells. All the new students, about sixty in all, and all girls, were assembled in the Winter Gardens waiting to be processed (Figure 2). We were given our uniforms, ordered previously from Rawcliffe's in Leeds. We had three sets of aprons and overalls - a check one for food preparation, a heavy

Figure 2. The Winter Gardens. *Bradford College*

green denim for heavy household tasks and pale green overalls for practical lectures. Each student had a number and all her culinary equipment was stamped accordingly. I was K54. We also were allocated rooms and room-mates at this session, which when complete meant you were able to be escorted to your new 'home' by a third-year student. My room had views over the moor towards White Wells and I looked out over the dismal snow-covered scene with trepidation as I awaited the late arrival of my room mate.

We were expected to dress for dinner, so I began to unpack my suitcase and chose something warm to wear. It was getting quite dark when the door opened to reveal my room-mate, her mother, father and dog. She had innumerable suitcases and boxes of food which her mother insisted on unpacking. The room soon became a scene of utter chaos as the gong rang for dinner. She decided to eat in our room so I went down alone to join the throng below. Some 160 students were milling around in the foyer whilst members of staff marshalled us into sixes and allocated us to tables in the dining room. The meal was very civilised, each student proudly clutching a brand new napkin and ring bought specially for college and ticked off on the 'requirements' list. We served each other going to the refectory staff for the relevant dishes following prayers, said by the principal, Miss Harding. The second and third years chatted away during the meal whilst we first years sat quietly observing the alien

Figure 3. Dining-Room. *Bradford College*

scene. I hated it. I already wanted to go home. I was homesick and felt very alone. I was seventeen years old and had not been away from home for any length of time before. (Figure 3)

The next day lectures began at 9.00am following breakfast which was an informal sitting. I began chatting to a girl from Warrington and we found that we were in the same groups. We had a mid-morning break when coffee was served in the Winter Gardens; around mid-afternoon tea would be served in the same venue. This time we would be given tea and huge trays of bread liberally covered with salt and beef dripping. This was devoured in record time as we hungry students pounced on it. I had never eaten bread and dripping before that but soon acquired the taste! I was amazed at the volume of work and could see why our course took three years to complete.

We had lectures in education, English, chemistry, biology, art, needlework, cookery, laundrywork and housecraft, social studies, health education. We were also taught Scottish country dancing and deportment. These lectures went on all day with special lectures in the evening and on Saturday mornings on occasion. In the evenings we had several hours writing up lecture

Figure 4. Entrance foyer. *Bradford College*

notes and undertaking assignments. In the entrance foyer of the college were situated the two telephones supplying incoming and outgoing calls to the students (Figure 4). Each evening two students would man them, on a rota basis, and rush round the entire college to find each individual student as the calls came in. It was no easy task as the building was on three levels and there were also student rooms in the annexe and sick bay. The duty lasted three hours, after which you would stagger to bed exhausted (Figure 5).

As students we were responsible for the cleanliness and maintenance of the appearance of our rooms. Early Tuesday mornings, before breakfast, we would take our sheets to the laundry room, give them to Miss Rushforth, the housekeeper, and exchange them for newly laundered, starched ones. We would then go to breakfast, after which we had to make up our beds, hospital style, with mitred sheet corners and folded back top sheet. We would then clean our rooms including the sink. Room inspection would follow later, undertaken by a member of staff as we stood to attention by the side of our beds. Only then could we proceed to practical lectures as this was deemed part of the course. Our lecturers were very strict and had exceptionally high standards. Everything was meticulously inspected. Praise and criticism were unstintingly given as the occasion warranted. Practical lectures formed the central core of the course and took place in specialist practical rooms (Figure 6). We were taught laundrywork, cookery, home management and a multiplicity of skills. I remember early on in the course our lecturer was demonstrating the value of labour saving equipment. We were told that it was possible to load the new automatic washing-machines and leave them to complete their cycle whilst we undertook a task elsewhere in college. Before this the twin tub held sway and needed

Figure 5. Annexe and Sick Bay. *Bradford College*

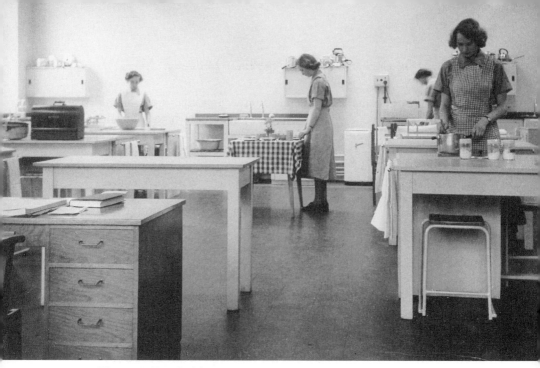

Figure 6. Practical lecture room. *Bradford College*

constant attention. The machines were loaded and we were told to return in an hour to see the results. At the designated time we walked along the main corridor and turned down by the dining-room. What a sight greeted us. The entire corridor along half its length was fast disappearing under a sea of foam as the four washing-machines completed their programme. The lecturer had not used automatic powder, as detergency of this type was still in its infancy and she had not foreseen the consequences. We all fell about laughing . Our tutor was furious and made us clean up all the mess. So much for labour saving devices!

Another important aspect of the course was the actual teacher training which necessitated visiting schools. My first real attempt at teaching took place in a large comprehensive school in Bradford. I showed the pupils how to set a table using the best linen and crockery as per Ilkley College. Later on my return to college my tutor sent for me to go to her rooms and asked me to evaluate my lesson. I felt quite pleased with my efforts until she pointed out that I had set the children impossibly high standards. Instead of starched linen I should have emphasised the importance of changing the table covering each meal. In their case this was the previous day's newspaper. My next teaching spell consisted of nine weeks in a different school. This meant that we had to live in 'digs' for that period, only returning to college at weekends for tutorials and lesson preparation. My friend, Norma, and I were to go to Mexborough, uncharted territory as far as we were concerned. We knew nothing of the mining communities and set off with an enthusiasm that was soon put to the test. Our billet was in Warmsworth, near Doncaster, and our hostess for the nine weeks was a diminutive, white-haired, jolly old lady, who welcomed us with open arms. There was a roaring coal fire blazing half way up the chimney, three well worn arm chairs in front of it and a kettle boiling away on the old fashioned range. Bliss. We were to experience some of the best home cooking I've ever tasted in the weeks spent with her.

We travelled by bus the next day to the secondary modern school at which we were to teach. The building was an austere Victorian structure alongside a main road. Inside it was very old-fashioned with high windows, scrubbed wooden tables, a mangle and a twin-tub washing-machine. At this time there were no mixed classes. Boys were taught wood and metalwork and girls did housecraft and needlework. I felt the beginning of a challenge when I met Mrs Moody, my supervising teacher. She was pleased to have me, she said, as it meant that she could catch the 3.30pm bus home instead of the one at 4.30pm! School was timetabled to end at 4.00pm but then there was all the day's clearing up to do. Cookery lessons in those days usually followed the same pattern. There would be a themed demonstration, and then the children would note the recipe bringing the ingredients the following week. My first theme was 'cheese', which I had carefully researched, making posters, display material and detailed lesson plans. I waited with trepidation to welcome my first class of the afternoon. These mining family lasses were very big girls who were in their final year at school and I would be less than honest if I said that I felt entirely confident with them. Their leader seemed very uneasy throughout the entire demonstration of the intricacies of macaroni cheese, and finally stood up as I asked them to copy the recipe for the following week. Arms akimbo she presented a formidable sight. 'You've got another think coming if you think we're mekkin' that muck,' she said 'it wain't go in our father's snap tin.' Mrs Moody was well on her way home by this time and no college tutor was available to help. We made cheese and onion pasties the next week, after all, teachers need to be versatile and improvise at times to survive, don't they? I learned to respect the children from Mexborough who were very self assured, down-to-earth, hardworking pupils, who, having made their views known taught me much about their close knit community life and their refusal to waste good money, as they saw it. They were not being cheeky merely outspoken. I learned a great deal about life in general at Ilkley which, in 1964, changed its name to Ilkley College of Education in preparation for the new degree courses due to start the following year. I left to start my teaching career in that year, a product of an excellent training establishment.

The college continued to train home economics teachers until 1982 when the Margaret McMillan College in Bradford merged with Ilkley College to become the Bradford and Ilkley Community College. The teacher training was to specialise in the field of general subjects and was to include the training of men! In 1993 the college diversified once more and became the Ilkley Community College Corporation and provided over 1,000 courses with 32,000 students from the UK and abroad enrolling every year. It was one of the largest providers of Further and Higher Education courses in the United Kingdom. Sadly the fortunes of the college changed and in the summer of 1999 Ilkley College closed. Its grounds are designated building land and the main building is to become luxury accommodation. It would seem that the history of Wells House, Ilkley has gone full circle.

Sources

The Ilkley Gazette.
Archive material from Ilkley College Corporation.
D. Carpenter, *Ilkley in the Victorian Era, 1980.*
J. Shuttleworth, *Guidebook to Ilkley and its neighbourhood.*
T.D. Luke, *Spas and Health Resorts of the British Isles, 1919.*
Leibold, G., *Practical Hydropathy. 1980*
A.B. Granville, *The Spas of England (Northern Division).*

Notes and References

1 *Ilkley in the Victorian Era.*
2 *Ilkley Gazette* 8.10.54.

Further Reading

R. Woodrow Thompson, *Ben Rhydding* (1867).
Ilkley Development Association. *Ilkley and Ben Rhydding - The Heather Spa* (1922).

6. HAWORTH CHURCHYARD: WHO WERE THEY?

by Ann Dinsdale

We've braved its ghosts often together, and dared each other to stand among the graves and ask them to come.... But Heathcliff, if I dare you now, will you venture? If you do, I'll keep you. I'll not lie there by myself; they may bury me twelve feet deep, and throw the church down over me, but I won't rest till you are with me... I never will!
Emily Brontë, '*Wuthering Heights*' (1847).

VISITORS TO HAWORTH PARSONAGE, the famous home of the Brontë family, are often struck by the melancholy churchyard, crammed full of graves, which surrounds the old house on two sides (Figure 1). When the poet Matthew Arnold visited Haworth in 1853 the churchyard must have made a striking impression on him, for when he came to write his elegy, *Haworth Churchyard*, shortly after Charlotte Brontë's death in 1855, he linked churchyard imagery with the Brontës' lives. Haworth Churchyard would certainly have made an appropriately gloomy resting-place for the Brontës, and Arnold (like many other visitors) was not pleased to discover that they had in fact been buried in a vault beneath the church floor. In a letter to Mrs Gaskell he wrote:

Figure 1. Haworth Parsonage and Churchyard before 1864, when trees were planted. *William Scruton Collection, Keighley Libraries.*

HAWORTH PARSONAGE.

I am almost sorry you told me about the place of their burial. It really seems to me to put the finishing touch to the strange cross-grained character of the fortunes of that ill-fated family that they should even be placed after death in the wrong, uncongenial spot.[1]

Although the burial registers for Haworth Churchyard go back to 1645, some of the gravestones pre-date this. It is usually claimed that 40,000 people are buried here, and a wander around the churchyard can tell you a lot about their lives. Gravestones often indicate a person's interests or occupation (look out for the graves of musicians decorated with musical scores or those of stonemasons showing the tools of their trade). They also indicate what an appallingly unhealthy place Haworth was in which to live. The Brontë story is well-known, but although the Brontës suffered, they did not suffer alone, for despite its hill-top setting and bracing moorland air, Haworth was an overcrowded and unhealthy place in which to live in the mid-nineteenth century.

In 1849 the villagers of Haworth sent a petition to the General Board of Health in London which resulted in an inspector, Benjamin Herschel Babbage, spending three days in Haworth to carry out an investigation into the water supply and sanitary conditions. In his report, published in 1850, Babbage estimated that the death-rate for Haworth was over 44 per cent higher than the neighbouring villages, and that every year almost twenty more people died in Haworth due to the appalling sanitary conditions[2] (Figure 2).

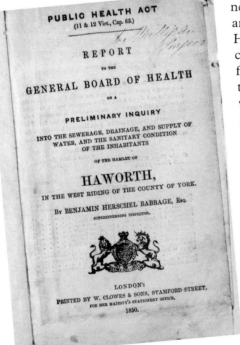

The majority of burials for the neighbouring villages of Oxenhope and Stanbury took place at Haworth, and the dreary churchyard was one contributing factor that helped to make Haworth the unhealthy place it was. Babbage was also worried about the way graves were covered by large flat stones:

The practice at Haworth is, to cover the grave with a flat stone, upon which is engraved the name, age, etc., of the dead; and the churchyard presents one entire surface of flat stones, laid at different heights from the ground,

Figure 2. The Babbage Report, 1850. *The Brontë Society.*

some of them simply reposing upon the mound of earth, which covers
the grave, whilst others are supported upon dwarf walls, and form
raised tombs...

It was a practice which he considered to be a 'very bad one', as the
flat tombstones prevented the growth of vegetation which would
have absorbed the gasses emitted during decomposition and made
the process less likely to contaminate the atmosphere. Babbage
recommended that the churchyard be closed, and that a new,
adequately drained site on the outskirts of the village would be,

the most efficacious means of diminishing the evils, which there can be
no doubt always take place from the vicinity of burial-grounds to
inhabited places.

There were two houses bordering upon the churchyard: the Parsonage
and the *Black Bull Inn*. In 1850 the Parsonage was the home of the
Reverend Patrick Brontë and his last surviving daughter Charlotte. A
great deal has been written about the Brontë family, and their fame has
ensured that every letter and scrap of information relating to them has
been preserved. This wealth of information can often be used to shed
light on the lives of their contemporaries in Haworth.

The majority of Charlotte Brontë's letters contain some reference
to Haworth's wild weather, and for those with constitutions already
weakened by poor living conditions and constant exposure to
infection and disease, the change of seasons could be a matter of life
or death:

... the cold here is dreadful. I do not remember such a series of North-
Pole days. England might really have taken a slide up into the Arctic
zone; the sky looks like ice; the earth is frozen; the wind is as keen as
a two-edged blade. We have all had severe colds and coughs in
consequence of the weather.... [3]

Shortly after her sister Emily's funeral, Charlotte wrote:

no need now to tremble for the hard frost and keen wind - Emily does
not feel them.

In *The Life of Charlotte Brontë*, published in 1857, Elizabeth Gaskell
wrote of the hardship suffered during one particularly bad winter:

But this winter of 1833-4 was particularly wet and rainy, and there
were an unusual number of deaths in the village. A dreary season it
was... the passing and funeral bells so frequently tolling, and filling the
heavy air with their mournful sound - and, when they were still, the

'chip, chip' of the mason, as he cut the grave-stones in a shed close by.

Elizabeth Gaskell had probably taken her information from Charlotte Brontë's letter of 11 February 1834, where she wrote:

what a remarkable Winter we have had! Rain and wind continually but an almost total absence of frost or snow ... with us an unusual number of deaths have lately taken place.

Local sources confirm that the weather was very wet and windy (only three days without rain were recorded in January 1834), but although the number of deaths was high, it was not unusually so.[4] On the very day Charlotte wrote the letter her father had conducted the funerals of five-year-old Mark Briggs and six-year-old Sarah Feather, and amongst the other child victims of that winter were Sarah and Elizabeth Binns, aged one and two years, who had both died on Christmas Day 1833.

Infant mortality was extremely high in Haworth: in the 1840s forty-one per cent of children born there died before reaching the age of six. In his 1850 report Babbage commented:

It is lamentable to think that so large an amount of infantile mortality should have been taking place year after year, unknown and unheeded, the inhabitants of Haworth being quite unaware of it... where this amount of infantile mortality prevails, who shall picture the mother's anxious care for her drooping offspring, the father's hard tasked labour to provide his family with the needful food and medicines, and the amount of pain and sorrow and disease, which the surviving children have to struggle through, before they get beyond this fatal epoch, and acquire an average chance of life.

There are many gravestones commemorating the deaths of these young children, one of the most visually poignant being that of the Heaton family. Six small brothers and sisters are buried here along with their parents, the gravestone lovingly carved by the children's father and ornamented with the replica of a sleeping baby which is said to represent his son James Whitham, who died aged one. The baby's arms are often filled with wild flowers, placed there by visitors moved by the sad story. It's quite common to find whole families of little children unnamed on their gravestones. Bernard Hartley died in 1841 and buried with him are 'eleven children of his who all died young'. The gravestone of Thomas and Mary Barraclough of Haworth records the deaths of five of their children. The children all go unnamed but the Barraclough family Bible has been preserved at

Figure 3. A plaque inside Haworth Church, commemorating the Brontë family. *The Brontë Society.*

the Brontë Parsonage Museum, and contains a loving record of the time and date of each child's birth and death. The oldest child, Zerrubabel, survived into his sixth year, while the youngest, Frances, was just ten months old. Another grave contains the seventeen children of Joseph and Mary Leeming of Keighley, the eldest of whom survived into his sixth year.

Readers of Emily Brontë's *Wuthering Heights* are often shocked by Heathcliff's brutal treatment of his dying son:

> *… None here care what becomes of him; if you do, act the nurse; if you do not, lock him up and leave him.*

In fact many of the causes of death in Haworth were recorded as 'unknown'. At the time Emily was writing her novel it was estimated by Babbage that 21.7 per cent of Haworth's population died without receiving any medical attention, and that this fact afforded

> *very great facility for the concealment of crime, ranging from murder in its naked form, through the various finely shaded gradations of ill-treatment, starvation, and neglect…*

The Sagar grave serves as a good example of just the kind of concerns Babbage had in mind. John Sagar was accused of having poisoned his wife, and at his trial at York Assizes in 1858, it was suggested that his eight children, buried in a single grave at Haworth, might not all have died from natural causes. Much of the magistrates' evidence was ruled inadmissible and the case eventually collapsed.

Anne was the only Brontë who was not buried in the family vault (she died in Scarborough and was buried there). When Patrick Brontë died in 1861, the graveyard had already been formally closed for five years and it was necessary to obtain permission from the Secretary of State before he could be interred inside the church. An

Figure 4. Tabitha Aykroyd was buried near the garden wall of the Parsonage. *The Brontë Society.*

Order in Council dated 1857 had reserved Patrick Brontë's right to be buried with his family, on condition that the coffin was imbedded in a layer of powdered charcoal and separately entombed in brick or stone.[5] (Figure 3). Outside in the graveyard the old Haworth names of Binns, Feather, Greenwood, Hartley, Heaton and Holmes abound. Here lie many of the Brontës' friends and neighbours.

Figure 5. Tabitha Aykroyd's grave. *The Brontë Society.*

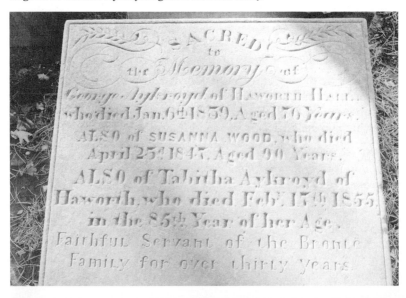

Buried close to the wall at the bottom of the Parsonage garden is Tabby Aykroyd, who went to work at the Parsonage when she was in her fifties (Figures 4 and 5). Tabby was described in *The Life of Charlotte Brontë* as a

> *thorough specimen of a Yorkshire woman of her class, in dialect, in appearance, and in character... Her words were far from flattery; but she would spare no deeds in the cause of those whom she kindly regarded.*

Tabby arrived at the Parsonage shortly after the deaths of the two eldest children, Maria and Elizabeth, and must have been a comforting presence to the motherless children. Tabby died at the age of eighty-four, just a few weeks before Charlotte in 1855.

Close to the south wall of the Parsonage garden is the Brown memorial (Figure 6). John Brown (1804-1855) lived opposite the churchyard in a house adjoining the Sunday school. By day, he was a stonemason and sexton at Haworth Church, but by night he took on the

Figure 6. The Brown's family grave, close to the south wall of the Parsonage garden. *The Brontë Society.*

more sinister role of Worshipful Master of the local Masonic Lodge, to which Branwell Brontë was initiated in 1836. John Brown was a close friend of Branwell's, though his influence may not always have been beneficial. Branwell's biographer, Francis Leyland, wrote:

> *It was, indeed, unfortunately, no infrequent circumstance to see.... Branwell listening to the coarse jokes of the sexton of Haworth - the noted John Brown - while that functionary was employed in digging the graves so often opened in the churchyard, under the shadow of the parsonage* [6] (Figure 7).

One of John Brown's daughters admitted that her father 'liked his glass' and was partly to blame for 'leading young Branwell on.' However, John

Brown was a great admirer of Branwell's talents, and according to another biographer, Mrs Chadwick, 'No one was more sorry, when Branwell died, than the Haworth sexton'.[7] A poem called *The Haworth Sexton* by a local poet Joseph Hardaker, was probably written with John Brown in mind:

> *O, Sexton! ye are such a soul,*
> *Ye little care for whom ye toll,*
> *If ye can drain the arvill bowl;*
> *With many more,*
> *Ye'll for a moment sigh and growl,*
> *Then all is o'er.*
>
> *Before the corpse, in solemn pace,*
> *Full oft I've seen ye pull a face,*
> *As though ye were to truth and grace*
> *Nearly allied;*
> *That few would think ye mean or base*
> *So deep ye sighed.*
>
> *But think ye, old case-hardened blade,*
> *Knight of the mattock and the spade,*
> *Some lustier brother of the trade,*
> *Perhaps ere long,*
> *May lig you where you've thousands laid,*
> *Nor think it wrong.*

Brown died in 1855 at the age of fifty-one from dust on the lungs. His brother William took over the job of sexton, also developing a sideline in entertaining early enthusiasts with his Brontë anecdotes. Among the other members of the Brown family to be buried here are John's daughter Martha (1828-1880), who was for many years a servant in the Brontë household, and his only son, John William, who died in his first year. When Brown's two-year-old granddaughter (also buried here) fell ill and died, while her mother was away from home, the sad task of informing her by letter fell to the elderly Patrick Brontë:

Figure 7. Portrait of John Brown, sexton of Haworth, by Branwell Brontë. *The Brontë Society.*

This is a sorrowful world, and I write to you on a sorrowful subject, you have already been informed that little Jane was in the scarlet fever; after some time, it was hoped she was recovering, and the danger was past. However, she rather suddenly got worse; and yesterday, and this morning things took an unfavourable turn, and she got worse, and worse, till at last she seemed to sleep away, till she closed her eyes on time, and opened them in eternity... [8]

Another familiar figure of the Brontës' Haworth was William Wood (1808-1889), the aptly named village joiner and cabinetmaker. In his workshop on the second floor of his home in Lodge Street, William made articles of furniture for the Brontës, including several of their coffins. According to his obituary in the *Bradford Observer*,

Whenever any notability visited Haworth in search of information relative to the Brontës – and there have been many both from America and other countries – Billy Wood was always sent for, and many are the times that he has been entertained at the Black Bull Hotel *by visitors.*

Three years after setting up practice in Haworth, Amos Ingham (1827-1889) was called on to attend his most famous patient, Charlotte Brontë. There was nothing that Dr Ingham or anyone else could have done to save Charlotte, and much to his lasting regret, Charlotte died on 31 March 1855. In 1870 Dr Ingham built himself one of the most attractive houses in Haworth, *Ashmount*, possibly financed by an inheritance from his father-in-law. In keeping with the gothic splendour of *Ashmount*, Dr Ingham's gravestone is one of the more ornate in the churchyard (Figure 8).

Mouldering in an overgrown corner of the graveyard lies the tomb of John Bateman Wheelhouse, the Haworth surgeon, and a mystery lies buried with him. Wheelhouse inspired a vicious poem by Branwell Brontë:

... him whose name begins with Wheel
and ends with House - Oh may he feel
His addled brains like molten lead
Anthony's fire blaze in his head
St Vitus dance distort each limb
His ears be deaf his eyes be dim
His tongue but move to curse his fate. [9]

The poem appears to reflect Branwell's

Figure 8. Dr Amos Ingham of Haworth. *The Brontë Society.*

Figure 9. The funeral card of Patrick Branwell Brontë. *The Brontë Society.*

jaundiced view in the last bitter months of his life, and when he died in September 1848, it was the much loathed doctor who signed his death certificate. Wheelhouse survived Branwell by less than four years, dying from dropsy at the age of thirty-two. Bearing in mind his early age at death, there is a strong possibility that this could have been caused by excessive drinking, shedding an interesting light on the man believed to have made himself hateful to Branwell Brontë by forbidding every form of intoxicant.[10]

Although alcoholism certainly contributed to Branwell Brontë's death at the age of thirty, consumption of beer and spirits in Haworth is said to have been considerably below average. In the late 1840s the village was served by three beer shops and seven public houses, several of these within a stone's throw of the church and a source of great annoyance to the Reverend John Wade who succeeded Patrick Brontë as Perpetual Curate in 1861. In a letter written to the Church Commissioners in 1866, Wade complained that:

> ... the inside of the gateway, being contiguous with an Inn is hardly better than a public urinal ... the steeple of the church, standing close to one of the paths is defiled in the same way.[11]

Life and Death in Haworth

Living conditions in Haworth were cramped and squalid, and Babbage noted that:

> *... from one end of the town to the other, I found the same deficient accommodation in the nature of back yards and privies... and the same want of ventilation in the sleeping-rooms of the poorer classes; all of them evils which powerfully tend to induce an unhealthy state in any population which may be unfortunate enough to be exposed to them.*

Many of those from the poorer classes lived in an area known as Brandy Row. While health improvements to Haworth came about only slowly in the years after Babbage's report, this area (now demolished) seems to have been the last to benefit. In a report published by the Civic Trust, over one hundred years after Babbage, the houses were described as being 'technically unfit'. The report goes on to add that one block had 'only one exterior lavatory for three houses.'[12] Conditions were crowded in Haworth for both the living and the dead:

> *According to the return furnished to me by the parish clerk, it would appear that 1,344 burials have taken place there during the last 10 years. Had these interments been ordered according to proper sanitary arrangements, they would have required a space of about eight-tenths of an acre, or nearly the entire area of the present churchyard.*

If Babbage's estimation was correct, then bearing in mind that the burial registers for Haworth Churchyard date back to 1645 provides some indication of the extent to which it was overcrowded. Despite Babbage's recommendation that the churchyard should be closed immediately, burials continued to take place, though after 1850 the churchyard was enlarged by the addition of a strip of land on the southern side. It wasn't until the 1890s that a new cemetery was opened on the edge of the moors.

Wandering round the graveyard at Haworth brings the dead to life, and behind each inscription can lie a tragic tale. Close to the Brown memorial is a gravestone commemorating Elizabeth Hartley who lost her life when the steamship *London*, bound for Australia, foundered in the Bay of Biscay on 11 January 1866. Of the 281 passengers who set sail, only eleven survived.

The Heatons of Ponden Hall were traditional trustees of Haworth Church and one of the more influential families in the area. Oral tradition suggests that the Heatons and Brontës were on friendly terms, and even that certain incidents in the Heaton family history contributed to Emily Brontë's *Wuthering Heights.* There are several tales of past Heaton tragedies, one concerning an attempted usurpation of the family fortunes by Henry Casson, a Heathcliff-like figure. Another story which was probably familiar to the Brontës concerned seventeen-year-old Elizabeth Heaton who married John Bakes in 1813. The young couple set up shop in Gomersal, but it appears that while Elizabeth was left to run the unheated shop, her husband spent his time at the local alehouse. Elizabeth became ill with tuberculosis and returned to Ponden taking her baby daughter with her. Her drunken husband continued to plague the family at Ponden, demanding her return, but she died on 12 March 1816, aged just twenty. Elizabeth's daughter, Eliza Matilda Bakes, died not long after, in January 1817 aged twenty-two months and was buried with her mother in Haworth Churchyard.[13]

Figure 10. Haworth Churchyard in the time of the Brontës.. *The Bookman, 190*

Though tragic, the Brontës' early deaths were clearly not unique in a village where the average life expectancy of 25.8 years matched that of some of the most unhealthy districts of London. Health improvements to Haworth, for which Patrick Brontë had campaigned, came too late to benefit his own family, and the many gravestones at Haworth stand as sad reminders of the suffering which was commonplace in the Brontës' day (Figure 10).

Notes and References

1 Tillotson, Kathleen, 'Haworth Churchyard: the making of Arnold's Elegy', *Brontë Society Transactions*, 15.77.105 (1967).

2 Babbage, *Report to the General Board of Health*, 1850.

3 Gaskell, Elizabeth, *The Life of Charlotte Brontë*, Oxford University Press, 1996, p.249.

4 This information is taken from Abraham Shackleton's manuscript weather records and cited by Margaret Smith in her edition of *The Letters of Charlotte Brontë Volume One*, 1829-1847, Clarendon Press, 1995, note 2, p.126.

5 Hirst, J.C., 'The Burial Place of the Brontës', *Brontë Society Transactions* 9.48.181 (1938).

6 Leyland, Francis A., *The Brontë Family with special reference to Patrick Branwell Brontë*, 2 Vols, Hurst and Blackett, 1886, Vol I, p.116.

7 Chadwick, Mrs Ellis H., *In the Footsteps of the Brontës*, Sir Isaac Pitman & Sons, 1914.

8 Patrick Brontë letter to Eliza Brown, 10 June 1859.

9 For the complete text of the poem see Neufeldt, Victor A., *The Poems of Patrick Branwell Brontë*, Garland Publishing, 1990, p.298.

10 Dinsdale, Ann, '"The most hated figure in Haworth": Doctor Wheelhouse', *Brontë Society Transactions* 23.2.178 (1998).

11 Wilks, Brian, 'The State of Haworth Churchyard', *Brontë Society Transactions* 23.1.71 (1998).

12 The Civic Trust, *Haworth: A Study of the Historic Village*, 1964.

13 Fermi, Sarah, 'A "Religious" Family Disgraced: New Information on a Passage Deleted from Mrs Gaskell's *Life of Charlotte Brontë*', *Brontë Society Transactions* 20.5.290 (1992).

7. IMPRISONED FOR THEIR CONSCIENCE: KEIGHLEY'S ANTI-VACCINATION PROTEST

by Pauline Barfield

DURING THE NINETEENTH CENTURY KEIGHLEY grew from a small village nestling on the banks of the River Worth to an important industrial town producing businessmen of international status. Looking at Keighley today it is hard to believe that it held such a position, the only clue being the fine buildings of North Street, the Town Hall, the Education Buildings and, although of a later date, the public library - the first Carnegie library in England.

In 1876 Keighley hit the national headlines in a story of deeply held beliefs and the determination of a group of men to take the consequences of upholding them. It is a story that contains farce and tragedy, heroes and villains and a chorus of townspeople booing and cheering. I first heard this story from a health researcher who was studying vaccination in the nineteenth century. It caught her imagination just as it caught mine and, by one of those strange coincidences that seem to happen with remarkable regularity, copies of letters written by one of the participants were sent to Keighley Reference Library by his great-granddaughter and it became a tale which just had to be told.

In 1796 Edward Jenner (1749-1823) made the first successful vaccination against smallpox using the cowpox virus. This was a great leap forward in the fight against one of the most dreadful diseases of the eighteenth and nineteenth centuries. Smallpox killed 20 per cent of its victims and permanently scarred or blinded the survivors. During the 1800s many countries passed laws requiring vaccination, but the vaccine was often of poor quality and the vaccination unsuccessful.

The population of Keighley had grown from 5,748 in 1801 to 18,259 in 1851 and like many northern industrial towns, the number of houses had not been able to keep up with this rapid growth. The influx of Irish immigrants at this time also added to the overcrowding of certain areas such as Westgate, Pinfold, Baptist Square and Turkey Street.

The Ranger Report (1855)[1] into the conditions in the town makes grim reading:

Turkey Street - *A very large number of pigstyes, manure heaps and other filthy and nauseous places.*

Back Turkey Street - *For the want of eaves point, etc. to the property of the trustees, the water from the buildings ran into the houses adjoining and below the level of this property, which makes the old property wet and almost unfit for habitation. Sickness in the family continually.*

Leeds Street - *Boils bellies and other animal matter for pigs in a room under a dwelling house, under the window of which is a pigstye and manure heap, very filthy.*

Mill Hill - *At the end of the house occupied by James Romley is a foul, stinking nauseous nuisance, a sumphole or tank which receives the contents of Romley's privy, slops and eaves water....*

No wonder disease was rife among the poor of the town when conditions such as these prevailed. Interestingly, this slum area was not demolished until the 1930s when Guard House Estate was built to replace it.

The Ranger Report recommended the setting up of a Local Board of Health and in 1855 it had twenty-one members who appointed Finance, Lighting and Watch Committees, an Inspector of Nuisances, Superintendent of Police and a Rate Collector!

It was obvious that something had to be done to stop the spread of disease and the government had passed the *Vaccination Acts* of 1840 and 1853 making it compulsory to vaccinate infants against smallpox, the cost to be met out of the local poor rate. Enforcement was limited and further acts were passed in 1867 and 1871 which included a fine of 25 shillings or imprisonment for parents who refused. There was much opposition to these measures, which were feared by many people, particularly the poor, as an unwelcome intrusion of state control into family life and the National Anti-Compulsory Vaccination League was set up to fight the law. The Keighley branch was formed and many influential members of the community joined. Its object was to spread knowledge about vaccination by means of literature and public meetings and in this it had the support of the *Keighley Herald*, a local weekly newspaper, which printed handbills at its office and advertised meetings for them. The League also defended members prosecuted under the Vaccination Acts and paid their fines. It also endeavoured to get its members elected to the Local Board of Guardians, as they were the body who had to enforce the laws. By 1873 the League was well

Figure 1. Keighley Guardians, 'Imprisoned for their Conscience'. *Keighley Photographic Society.*

established. The *Keighley News*[2] of Saturday 8 February 1873 reported:

A largely attended meeting of the Anti-Compulsory Vaccination League was held on Thursday evening at the Lyceum, Low Street, Keighley. After some discussion as to the course that ought to be pursued with reference to the prosecution for non-compliance with the act, it was resolved to make strenuous efforts at the ensuing election of Guardians to stay legal proceedings, which the League look upon in the light of persecution... all fines and costs will be paid by the society on payment of sixpence per month.

The League succeeded in getting members Messrs. Newbould, Tempest, Sedgwick and Milner elected, the most prominent being Robert Alsop Milner who was made Chairman of the Board. Born in 1840, he had married Gulielma Smith on 15 April 1868 and settled in Carlisle. By 1871 they had moved to Keighley and, according to the census, he had set up a business in Low Street as a tailor and outfitter. By 1876 they had three children - Alicia (1869), Isabel (1871), Wilfred (1875) and Gulielma was expecting Felix who was born in December 1876. At this time they were living at Utley Green Head. They were devout Quakers.

In 1876 things came to a head.

Arrest of Keighley Guardians - Great Excitement

This was the headline of the *Keighley Herald* on 12 Saturday of August 1876.

At last the 7 rebellious Guardians of the Keighley Union are under arrest (Figure 1).

Two columns of newsprint told the tale, which, summarised, was that a *mandamus* had been issued by the Court of Queen's Bench to compel them to implement the *Vaccination Act* but eight of the Guardians refused to obey it. The Local Government Board was then granted a

writ of attachment against Messrs R.A. Milner (chairman), J.B. Sedgwick, Titus Ogden, John Jefferey, Hezekiah Tempest, David Normington, James Newbould, and Samuel Johnson. When the mention of attachment, however, was made, Mr Johnson... promised obedience and pleaded ignorance of the effect of his vote, and the Lord Chief Justice held that he had freed himself from the writ of attachment.

The Guardians were then arrested for contempt of court.

On Thursday 10 August Mr Jefferey had the distinction of being the first Guardian to be arrested. He was a carrier by trade from Harden who attended the weekly market at Bradford every Thursday. As he walked off the station in Bradford he was stopped by a police officer who arrested him, took him into custody from which he 'was conveyed per Great Northern Railway via Leeds to York Castle' (*Keighley Herald*, 12 August).

The news slowly spread to Keighley where Robert Milner 'the most inveterate misdemeanant of the whole' rode over to Harden to confirm with Mrs Jefferey the true situation, but she could only state that her husband had not returned from Bradford. The other six Guardians spent Thursday evening putting their affairs in order in preparation of imminent arrest.

Friday 11 August dawned and the townsfolk of Keighley were agog to see what events the day would bring. First, two sheriff's officers, George Chambers and H.K. Whally, arrived on the 9.56am train with Edward Dobson, police officer, and a large detachment of assistants. Within half an hour of their arrival the first arrest had been made. The *Keighley Herald* [3] relates the events thus:

About quarter-past ten o'clock Mr Milner, the chairman of the Board, and perhaps the strongest opponent of the Acts, was coming down to business (accompanied by Mrs Milner), from his house at Utley Green Head, just as the officers arrived at the court-house. Mr Milner was proceeding down Bow Street to go via Cooke Lane to his shop in Low Street, when Mr Whalley and Mr Dobson were heard behind shouting 'Heigh'. Mr Milner turned round, and then proceeded a few steps, when the same cry of 'Heigh' came from the same quarter. A stand was made and the two officers coming up, a very short and business-like conversation followed.

Mr Whalley: Mr Milner, I believe, aren't you?

Mr Milner: Yes sir; that is my name.

Mr Whalley: You are wanted, you know, I attach you in the name of the Queen.

Mr Milner: All right, gentlemen, I shall offer you no opposition, I assure you. I suppose you will allow me to go to my shop for my letters?

Mr Whalley: Oh, certainly.

Mr Milner: I suppose you will take us altogether now.

Mr Whalley: Well, that depends on how many we get...

It was then arranged to proceed to Mr Milner's place of business... The news of Mr Milner's arrest spread rapidly over the town and within minutes of the time when he and the officers entered his shop a large crowd had assembled outside. A short time afterwards, the officers set actively to work and the next capture they made was that of Mr Titus Ogden, whose shop is a little higher up the street than Mr Milner's. Just as Mr Ogden was leaving his shop he was 'attached' and was subsequently taken to Mr Milner's place of business. At this point Mr Milner suggested to the officers that there would be no difficulty either about the arrests or the removal of the Guardians, so far as they themselves were concerned, and expressed a wish that they might be all conveyed to York together. He also suggested that they should be allowed to take dinner together, before leaving, and in consequence of the way in which the officers were met, this arrangement was at once acceded to.

Mr Sedgwick was the next to be arrested. He stopped work, gave instructions to his men and then proceeded to go home via the barbers for a shave. He then made his way to the Devonshire Hotel to meet the other Guardians for dinner. Another two police officers went further down the street and apprehended Mr Normington who also went home to 'get cleaned up' but this time his workmen followed hooting and shouting at the officers.

There were now only two Guardians left, Mr Tempest and Mr Newbould who owned a farm at Aiden, near Sutton. A 'conveyance' was sent for him and he immediately agreed to join his fellow Guardians so that they could all be transported to York together.

His wife, while bidding him good-bye in the heartiest manner, expressed a hope that those who had been the cause of his going might be vaccinated twice every morning and once every night as long as they lived'.

Mr Tempest had been working all morning before his arrest. The *Keighley Herald* continues the tale:

He seemed to have been the more contumacious than any of the others, for when arrested, he declined to walk a step towards prison. Mr William Smith, auctioneer, volunteered to use his influence to induce Mr Tempest to come with the officers, but Mr Tempest continued obstinate. Mr Smith then got a cab, and Mr Tempest had to be carried by the officers into the cab, and out of the cab into the hotel. Mr Smith afterwards offered to provide the Guardians with newspapers during their sojourn in prison.

Poor Mr Smith did not know what consequences his good deeds would have for himself as the day progressed.

By this time word of the events had spread through the town and, as the workers from the mills and workshops stopped for lunch, a crowd gathered in Church Green and the streets around the Devonshire Hotel. The police guarded the entrances to the hotel but as Mr Newbould was brought in via the back door fifty or more young men burst in through the gates and into the yard. As the time drew near for the Guardians to leave the policemen tried to clear the yard, unsuccessfully, until they started to write down the names of people they knew - a very effective method indeed. The Guardians could now leave in safety.

It was originally planned that the Guardians should walk to the station to catch the 1.45pm train to Leeds but the size of the crowd decreed that an omnibus would be more appropriate. Robert Milner appealed to the crowd not to interfere with their arrest. Hezekiah Tempest again refused to walk and was carried to the omnibus. The hotel gates were flung open and the omnibus set off at a cracking pace, scattering the crowd. Instead of taking the direct route to the station the omnibus went along Skipton Road and down Lawkholme Lane with half the crowd in tow. The other half thought the bus was going down Cavendish Street and so took that route arriving at the station before the Guardians. The Leeds train arrived and left before the Guardians could board it. By this time the crowd was so large they filled the platforms and blocked all the streets around the station. At this point the mood of the crowd began to change from the good humour which had prevailed so far. The *Keighley Herald* takes up the tale again:

> *A train for Bradford follows the Leeds train within a few minutes and the removal from Keighley might still have been effected by this train had not the crowd, which was rapidly gaining density, at once seized the horses, unharnessed them, lifted the top from the omnibus, and, the Bradford train having gone, proceeded to drag the conveyance with all its occupants, triumphantly up the street. The principal streets were traversed in this manner, the crowd cheering as they approached the residences or places of business of any of the Guardians. When the 'bus was being dragged down Coney Lane, towards Low Bridge, one of the officers, somewhat alarmed, asked where they were going now? One of his seniors significantly remarked 'To the beck'. True it was that they were proceeding in that direction, but as the turn was made towards the beck, another turn was made immediately afterwards, which somewhat allayed the feelings of alarm aroused in the minds of the officers, and the conveyance again took the road towards the town, via Longcroft.*

Enter William Smith, auctioneer, again. For some reason he had accompanied the Guardians and was in the carriage while all this was taking place. Several of the crowd objected to him being there and threatened to overturn the vehicle if he did not get out. As the omnibus approached the Mechanics' Institute he leapt out and made a dash for the curator's entrance, part of his coat-tails being ripped off in the process. He managed to enter the Institute but the crowd threw missiles and broke two of the windows. Later, when the crowd was dispersing,

> *a number of the rougher members of the assemblage adjourned to North Street, and congregated in front of the auction-rooms of Mr Smith, who had arrived there from the Mechanics Institute. Amid much shouting and yelling, a number of pieces of limestone, taken from a cart standing near, were thrown at the windows and some panes of glass were broken.*

Poor William Smith! I suspect he would not be in a hurry to help in the future.

At Robert Milner's suggestion it was agreed that the officers and Guardians should meet next morning at a prearranged time and be escorted to York. The omnibus stopped outside Mr Milner's shop in Low Street where Mr Milner and Mr Sedgwick mounted a balcony at an upper window and addressed the crowd to loud cheers, thanking them for their peaceful support and giving them another night of freedom. The crowd moved on to Titus Ogden's shop where he, also, made a speech thanking them for the orderly manner in which they had behaved.

The *Keighley News* roundly condemned the Guardians and the crowd for their actions:

> *There seems to be no end to the lawlessness which is to arise out of the anti-vaccination agitation. Keighley people have reason to be ashamed of the anti-legal demonstration of yesterday. It is no use mincing matters. The spectacle of a mob rendering impossible the carrying out of the law is always a disgrace... . The Guardians themselves came very well out of the affair; and strongly as we have opposed their conduct, and righteous as we believe the action of the law to be, we heartily recognise the sensible way in which they did their best to prevent the affair from becoming more serious...[but] They, as Guardians, refused to allow the Vaccination Laws to be put in force. They became Guardians for that very purpose.... If each man is to be the judge as to what laws he will obey and what laws he will disobey,*

Figure 2. The Debtor's Prison, York. *Architecture of York.*

> *the mob yesterday was in the right, and would be in the right if it broke*
> *windows, or for that matter the head of every man in Keighley who is*
> *in favour of the Vaccination Law. We earnestly ask them to consider the*
> *very dangerous tendency of their course of action. They see the natural*
> *result which follows whenever the supremacy of the law is disputed.*[2]

Strong words indeed which certainly showed which side of the argument the *Keighley News* supported. If the *Keighley News* was pro-vaccination then the *Keighley Herald* definitely supported the Anti-Vaccinationists.

The good folk of Keighley had to wait until the following Saturday, 19 August, to read the sequel to the tale as both newspapers were published weekly. There was a small crowd of about 300 in Keighley to see the Guardians board the train to Leeds and thence to York and the Debtor's prison - not Clifford's Tower as the press and popular verse had it (Figure 2).

There were supporters waiting to cheer them on at Leeds Station including some prominent Anti-Vaccinationists from the city. The crowd exhorted them to 'stand firm' and 'never give in' to which one of the Guardians replied 'No fear we are going for right against might' The people of York were indifferent to their plight. On the following Monday they were in trouble for sending a political manifesto to supporters in Leeds and the justices banned them from doing so again and from receiving any books, papers and pamphlets on vaccination 'Lest they should be confirmed in their contumacy' it was also reported 'that they purchase their own food, and according to a gentleman who has just visited them, they are as happy as the day is long'. They had visits from prominent Anti-Vaccinationists including the president of the National Anti-Vaccinationists League. They were sent gifts of fruit, books and a fund was set up for their defence (Figure 3).

The 26 August edition of the *Keighley News* under the heading 'Keighley Martyrs' roundly condemned their actions with a particular attack on Robert Milner and his Quaker beliefs.

> *A Quaker who was made a general against his will might have made some claim on our sympathies if he refused to lead his army into battle. But what should we say of a Quaker who solicited the appointment of general for the express purpose of paralysing the action of the troops of which he had asked to have the command?*

The *Keighley Herald* reported meetings of support where guest speakers proclaimed with great rhetoric the evils of vaccination and their admiration for the stand the guardians had made. On 9 September, the *Keighley Herald* printed a biography of Robert Milner. He was born at Hanley in Staffordshire into a family of Quakers but was brought up in Stockport. He attended the Quaker school at Ackworth near Pontefract and set up business with his brother Thomas when he was twenty-one. He supported the temperance movement and the Peace Society. His wife came from Thirsk and it was with the birth of their first child that they became interested in the vaccination question. He became a strong campaigner against vaccination and he was arrested and fined firstly in July 1871, a year after he had settled in Keighley, and again the following year

Figure 3. A defence fund was immediately set up. *Keighley Library.*

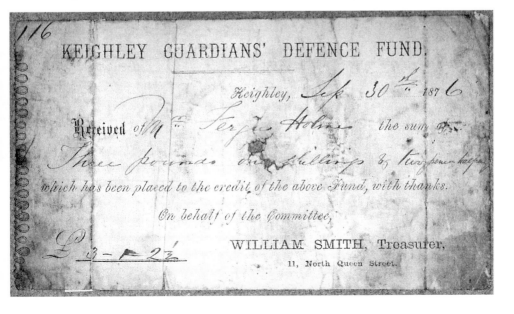

when he was fined 20s and costs. The Anti-Compulsory Vaccination League had grown in strength and in 1874 put forward Robert Milner and the others as candidates for election to the Local Board of Guardians. The following year they had a majority and Robert was elected chairman. The paper describes them as

these courageous and self-sacrificing men are not only suffering on behalf of Keighley, but for the whole country... . They are standing up for parental rights, the demands of conscience, and the first principles of human liberty (Figure 4).

Recently letters from Robert to his wife have come to light[4]. These were censored by the prison but still show a different aspect of life in prison. Robert writes on the 20 August:

Figure 4. Robert Alsop Milner. *Keighley Library.*

The Governor has sent us bibles - a great number of bound volumes of the penny magazines and quite a library of the 'Silly Series' of books quite new, so that we shall have an abundance of reading. This morning he very kindly sent over a splendid cucumber out of his garden. Nothing can exceed the kindness of everybody. We 'live in a land of pure delight where pleasures banish pain' - not greater delights though than Utley Green Head and the company of all you nice people - but that is forbidden fruit. Today for the first time we have ceased to be locked in our rooms - only on this floor which contains our suite of apartments.

23 August 1876:

My Dear Skylark,
Last night five of us purged our contempt for bad meat. Tempest and Ogden however must remain in prison till they have reduced their tough stomachs to human frailty. Sedgwick was and is very poorly. But the rest are better. This afternoon I am better than I have been all along I think.

We have had this a.m. Greenwood, Lonsdale, Lancaster and Mr Laycock of Bradford to see us. Yesterday Councillor Kenworthy and another gentleman from Leeds called to see us....

3.30pm since writing the above Councillor White of Leeds, Dawson of Sheffield and others from Glasgow, Keighley, Dewsbury and Heckmondwike etc. quite a little crowd have called.... .

I do not forget our little lasses but often remember them and pray for them and all of you.... .

If we stay until November [the time set for their hearing] I wish that it could be arranged to have someone to buy our requirements and cook for us. I am sure we could do it much more healthfully and comfortably.

Thy own 'Curlew'

4 September 1876 York Monday afternoon:

My dear Gulie,

Gulie's Daily Post is always the best daily newspaper I receive and is always interesting.... .

Yesterday evening I had a great pain in my right chest - something of a congestion. I rubbed it in the best fashion I could and put on afresh my compress which I have on again today.... .

If we get bail it will be no thanks to the doctors. You may judge how strongly they feel against us when our own doctor Holman (if we have a doctor) said as we were coming out of the Devonshire, 'they ought to be horse-whipped down to the station'. I think I did not tell thee before.

Robert was still suffering with chest pains when he wrote again to Gulielma on 6 September. He had finished the letter when a vital piece of news arrived. He added this postscript:

4.00pm. Governor has just called us down. He has just returned from London where yesterday he waited on [the] LGB Home Office Sheriff and has got us bail. One reason mentioned was my health. I have just telegraphed to you and Leeds.

Bail was set at £2,000 for each Guardian and the Anti-Compulsory Vaccination League at once offered to put up the money. The Governor was quite relieved to see them released as their celebrity status had caused all sorts of problems. They had sent out messages to other anti-vaccinationist groups which put them further in contempt of court, several of them had to be banned from smoking and there had been a constant stream of visitors and sightseers. Robert Milner's health had also caused concern although, by the tone of his letters, it was a recurring condition.

Meanwhile, the remaining Board of Guardians had met and by

three members to two had decided to implement the law and make vaccination compulsory.

On Saturday 10 September Robert Milnes and his fellow protestors returned to Keighley to a hero's welcome, not unlike the manner in which they tried to depart! They were greeted by a large crowd which had gathered at the station, but this time the platforms were kept clear. Just as the train drew in it started to pour with rain but this did not deter the crowd and when the rain eased about half an hour later the Guardians boarded a wagonette which was drawn through the streets of Keighley by a group of young men, escorted by a brass band in front and another behind. They finished their journey at a piece of spare land on Halifax Road near St Peter's Church Mission and addressed a mass meeting.

The case of the Queen versus the Guardians of the Keighley Union came up at the High Court of Justice in November 1876. They were found guilty and promised not to rescind the decision of the Board. The case was closed as they were deemed to have purged their contempt. Nine days later they resigned from the Board.

In these days of universal vaccination against a variety of diseases and the eradication of smallpox it is hard to imagine such strength of feeling, yet there are issues today which arouse public passion. Eco-warriors and nuclear protesters are two groups who spring to mind as people who are willing to break the law and risk imprisonment for their beliefs. Also, it is not so long ago when there was a vociferous protest in the local press about adding fluoride to the drinking water. The spirit of the Keighley Guardians lives on and the townsfolk would rise again if there was an attempt to curtail their civil liberties.

Bibliography

1 Ranger Report into the sanitary conditions of Keighley 1855.
2 *Keighley Herald* - various editions between 12 August and 16 September 1876.
3 *Keighley News* 8 February 1873; 12 August - 16 September 1876.
4 Milner, R.A. *Letters from York Castle to his wife*, 1876.

Acknowledgements

Keighley Photographic Society for illustrations 1, 3 and 4.
Gee, Eric. *Architecture of York*, Cerialis Press, York, 1979 for illustration 2.

8. THE GLORY OF LISTER PARK: A CENTURY OF ENJOYMENT

by Peter Shutt

LISTER, OR MANNINGHAM PARK, on the north side of Bradford is, at first sight, just another open space in the heart of a sprawling city. It contains within its tree lined boundary a museum and art gallery, a lake, an area of tennis courts and bowling greens, and, in summer, a colourful display of bedding plants.

The Park certainly has a long history. It was once the site of Manningham Hall, the home of the Lister family. It is well recorded that, in 1870, Samuel Cunliffe Lister sold Manningham Park to the Bradford Corporation for the sum of £40,000, being only half of its true value. On 18 August, that same year, the Park was opened to the public for the first time (Figure 1).

After the sale of Manningham Park and Hall, Lister went to reside at Farfield Hall near Addingham. In 1873 he purchased Swinton Hall and estates eventually making this his home. In that same year

Figure 1. Manningham Park, 1873. *Brear's Guide to Bradford, 1873*

he was elevated to the peerage and took the title of Baron Masham of Swinton (Figure 2).

In May 1898, the now Lord Masham offered to build the Cartwright Memorial Hall on the site of his old home in Manningham Park at a cost of £40,000, the exact sum of money he had been paid by the Bradford Corporation when he sold the Park to them in 1870. The offer was accepted and the work commenced. The building, finally completed, was officially opened on Wednesday 13 April 1904.

By 1904 all were proud of Bradford's prosperity. On Wednesday 4 May their Royal Highnesses the Prince and Princess of Wales visited Bradford to open the Great Exhibition in Lister's Park. The manufacturing products of Bradford were proudly on display, treasures of art exhibited and all the fun of the fair

Figure 2. Samuel Cunliffe Lister, Baron Masham of Swinton. *Bradford Libraries.*

Figure 3. Bandstand, Lister Park, c1914. *Bradford Libraries.* This bandstand is later than the one referred to on page 98.

Figure 4. The water chute. *Peter Shutt.*

prevailed. There was something for everyone, a crystal maze, a palace of illusions, a gravity railway, a captive balloon, music from a band and choir and countless other attractions.

The Park now truly belonged to the people of Bradford.

Fred Rowe, later to become the foreman gardener, had been an apprentice at the Park at the turn of the century. He could recall the building of the Cartwright Hall and the Great Bradford Exhibition of 1904. He would speak of the strange Spanish lady who rode her horse side-saddle through the Park each morning, and of the rich bewhiskered top hatted gentlemen from the big houses in Emm Lane and North Park Road driving along in graceful carriage and pair. He described sights and scenes of nannies wheeling children in baby carriages on warm summer afternoons, and of the horse-drawn fire

Figure 5. The New Bridge. *Peter Shutt.*

Figure 6. The Exhibition Hall. *Peter Shutt.*

engine racing to a fire in a shop at the top of Victor Road.

In recalling the Great Exhibition he remembered the band concerts in the bandstand by the lake (Figure 3), the water chute (Figure 4), a crystal maze, a wonderful bridge spanning the lake beneath which gondolas and petrol launches sailed (Figure 5), a Somali village, ('a reight mucky 'ole'), a splendid Exhibition Hall (Figure 6), the gondola boathouse (Figure 7), innumerable trade

Figure 7. The Boat House. *Peter Shutt.*

Figure 8. The Industrial Hall. *Peter Shutt.*

halls (Figure 8) and, above all, the crowds! The Great Exhibition had been a magnificent event in the history of the Park and, indeed, in the history of Bradford.

After the close of the Exhibition many of its buildings were dismantled and sold, only a few remained. Mr Harry Hornby, later to become Chairman of Bradford Northern Football Club, bought much of the roofing lead as scrap. Gone was the bridge over the lake and the magnificent Exhibition Hall. The boathouse, the start of many a gondola trip, remained as a place where one might hire a rowing boat in later years. A wooden building below the Cartwright Hall, which had housed a trade exhibition for Van Houten's cocoa, became the Masham Cafe. The bandstand on the lakeside served as a shelter long after a new bandstand had been erected below the bowling greens. The Palace of Illusions found a new home and popularity at Sunnyvale Pleasure Gardens, near Hipperholme.

Between the wars it was customary on Sunday afternoons, weather permitting, for a family to go together for a walk. Children were discouraged from playing out in the streets, or making undue noise. Sunday School, followed by a Sunday walk was almost a ritual. Living as we did not far from the Park, we had a choice of walks, among them, Heaton Woods, Six Days Only, or to Grandma's in Girlington. The favourite for us and many other families, was a walk around Lister Park, perhaps to feed the ducks by the lake or visit the Cartwright Hall. I remember there being a lovely large model of a steam locomotive on display downstairs in the Cartwright and however many times I went to see it, I would still stand and gaze at it in fascination, until dragged away by, no doubt, bored parents.

Listening to the band concerts in the Park was also very popular during the summer, as well-known military bands and local brass bands regularly entertained during Sunday afternoons and evenings. Deckchairs were arranged on the grass, below the bowling greens, overlooking the bandstand and were readily occupied by the eager crowds. Regimental military bands drew the largest audiences, playing patriotic music, stirring marches and excerpts from Gilbert and Sullivan operas.

Walking home at the end of our family afternoon in the Park, we would walk back through the Botanical Gardens. It was always very quiet in there and we would meander round the maze of little pathways looking at the plants, all with strange Latin names. There was a palm tree at the lower end of the garden which was always embalmed in hessian sacking during the autumn and winter months but would be unveiled again in late spring to give the garden an almost tropical appearance during the summer. There was also a Liriodendron tree at the top of the garden. Malin Smith, the Park's botanist, explained that it was also known as a Tulip Tree, because of its tulip shaped leaves and flowers. Malin Smith looked after the botanical garden and was also a botany teacher and lecturer, during the evenings, at the Bradford Technical College. During weekdays he could often be found potting and taking cuttings in his small greenhouse near the botanical gardens. His knowledge of plants and fungi was legendary. During the autumn he would often make himself a lunch-time snack of soup made from plant and wild fungi, ingredients found growing in the Park.

During the school holidays, as children, we would venture down to the Park with friends, sometimes to paddle or sail boats on the children's paddling pool. Occasionally, on warm summer days, it was so crowded with other children that neither was possible. Instead we would follow the stream back alongside the Botanical Gardens almost to where it emerged from under a culvert and there create a small dam where we could sail our home-made boats in peace. These were the idyllic days of childhood.

The Park seemed a huge place, surrounded by ornate iron railings and guarded by tall heavy iron gates. The gates were kept locked between sunset and six or seven in the morning, depending on the time of year. Dogs and cycling were prohibited, 'keep off the grass' signs were everywhere and, just to ensure that all the rules were kept, the Park Ranger patrolled during opening hours. The Ranger, Douglas, was a tall, straight backed, ex-cavalryman from the First World War, with a voice that would rival any sergeant major's. It was not a voice that any misbehaving boy would dare to ignore. If we saw Douglas coming we would hide, just in case we had innocently been breaking some Park rule.

Tennis or bowls created only a passing interest but the swimming pool was something quite different. The old open air pool, a spartan place, surrounded by a high wooden fence had been replaced during the mid 1930's by a modern lido. Here, on warm summer days, we would queue to gain entrance, waiting patiently for 'our turn'. Once inside we were given a wire basket in which to place our clothing. We would then hand the basket over to the attendant who would give us a numbered token in exchange. 'Don't lose that lad, or you'll be going home in your cozzie' (swimming trunks), he would warn, as we rushed to join the others in the water. The pool always felt very cold, even on hot days. It wasn't long before we were blue and shivering but still determined to stay in the water for as long as we could.

After 1939 the Park began to change. With the threat of war looming we watched as men began digging air-raid trenches in sections of the large oval grass area below the Cartwright Hall. The doorways and entrances to the Cartwright Hall were protected by sandbags.

As the war started the iron railings surrounding the Park were removed as part of the war effort, leaving only the huge ornate gates in place. Curiously, throughout the whole of the war years, the gates were still locked at dusk each day and unlocked again each morning, thus maintaining the long established pre-war routine (Figure 9).

The new Bradford Boys' Grammar School building in Frizinghall

Figure 9. The gates and Cartwright Hall. *Peter Shutt.*

had just been completed at the outbreak of war and before the boys could move in, the army requisitioned it for the RASC. As the troops took over they parked their camouflaged vehicles round the carriage-ways of the Park. They drilled in front of and below the Cartwright Hall. Commissioned officers were billeted with families in houses on North Park Road and Victor Road. There were other changes too, for immediately within the gates at the bottom of Victor Road the AFS (Auxiliary Fire Service) built an emergency static water tank, to augment water supplies in the case of an air-raid. Tucked away behind the greenhouses a large hut provided quarters for a full-time Civil Defence Officer. The gardeners, one by one, were called up, to be replaced by Land Army girls.

At the start of the war Mr Moreby was Head Gardener (Figure 10). Just a few years before he had broken his back in an accident, from which he recovered, while assisting in the moving of the large statue of a stag behind the Cartwright Hall. Miss Cissie Clough, a former First World War Land Girl had stayed on at the Park and she described Mr Moreby as 'a bluff Yorkshireman, who never used a swear word.' In moments of utter frustration he would shout 'Manchester', which, I suppose to most Yorkshire folk would be the

Figure 10. Lister Park gardeners, c1930. *Bradford Heritage Recording Unit.*

Figure 11. Floral display c.1930. *Peter Shutt*

equivalent of swearing. If he was appointing a new apprentice he would invite the lad to his house for an interview and seated in his favourite rocking-chair, gently rocking to and fro, he would ask him 'Does t'a want to be a gardener?' When the answer came 'Yes', he would enquire 'Does t'a know abart logarithms?' The lad would reply hesitantly, that he had heard of them. Mr Moreby would then smile and begin rocking backwards and forwards in his chair ever more vigorously, suddenly saying, 'Tha can start Monday then.' The interview would be deemed to be over and Cissie would then show the lad round the range of greenhouses before sending him on his way, with a reminder to 'turn up promptly at 7.00am on Monday.' Mr Moreby died in the early 1940s leaving Fred Rowe as acting Head Gardener. Among the half a dozen Land Girls, his daughter Clara Moreby remained as a member of the war time gardening team. Clara, like her father, was a bluff Yorkshire character and would often be seen smoking a pipe as she worked, much to the astonishment of passers-by.

Pre-war the gardens had been dedicated to growing flowers, in particular the exotic and the unusual for display in the large Victorian conservatory. Outside and in front of the Cartwright Hall during the summer months the beds were a tailored display of intricate floral designs (Figure 11). Individual Bradford Parks vied to create the most elaborate carpet bedding and in one memorable year the gardeners created an arrangement in the shape of a huge grand piano!

With the advent of war all this changed. Food production became all important and the Bradford Parks Department was expected to do its share. The Land Girls helped to plant leeks and onions where once dahlias had flowered. The greenhouses were turned over to growing tomatoes, cucumbers and lettuce. Even so, the public was entitled to a little cheer and the grand Victorian Conservatory still housed palms and a display of flowers. Fred Rowe relished growing Schizanthus, the poor man's orchid plant, to an unbelievable size. Each single plant would be tended lovingly until it was between three and four feet square and supported by as many as sixty to seventy separate garden canes. These beautiful plants in nine or ten inch pots, completely covered in bloom, would be arranged on staging in the Conservatory for all to see. Chrysanthemums too, would take their place in season to delight and add a little colour during those drab wartime years.

The older gardeners took it in turns to 'firewatch' at the Cartwright Hall. Each evening two of the men would stay on duty overnight in the Hall. If the air-raid sirens sounded they patrolled the building in case a stray incendiary bomb should land on the building. Mercifully, to my knowledge, none ever did.

The traditional family holiday at the coast was, by now, for the most part, out of the question. Once familiar seaside holiday beaches were surrounded by barbed wire, mines, and pill-boxes. Wartime propaganda recommended staying at home. As a result, special 'Holiday at Home' weeks were arranged in the Park. A stage was erected by the bandstand and local artistes entertained. There was always a talent spotting competition when would-be comedians and singers would step hopefully onto the stage making a bid for stardom!

When the war ended the Park said goodbye to the faithful team of Land Army Girls. One by one the gardeners were demobilised from the forces and turned up in their grey, chalk or pin-stripe, demob suits seeking to be reinstated in their jobs. Fred Whiteley was one of their number and it was he who helped to introduce a whole new passion for the growing of Chrysanthemums (Figure 12). Great show blooms were the order of the day and competition between individual Parks flourished. Bradford combined the expertise of its several Parks and challenged other cities in regional shows. Sheffield, Leeds, Halifax and Huddersfield were all its rivals and some magnificent exhibitions were held each autumn throughout the area.

Fred Whiteley became well-known as a judge at the various local Chrysanthemum Society and Allotment Society annual shows. As ever, the display of blooms in Lister Park became one of the most noted and extravagant among all the Bradford Parks.

The lovely summer show of flowers in front of the Cartwright was, once again, as splendid as any seen in pre-war years. A garden for the blind, raised beds of aromatic plants and scented flowers, each labelled in Braille, was also built on an area of land above the lake.

People came in numbers to enjoy the Park. Boating on the lake drew many to take a trip on the motor launch or to hire a rowing-boat for half an hour. During August a fair visited with roundabouts swings and dodgems. The sounds of music and the shouts of excited

Figure 12. Chrysanthemums. *Peter Shutt.*

Figure 13. Lister Park Fair, 1975. *Telegraph & Argus.*

children echoed across the green (Figure 13). In winter, when the ice was thick on the lake and snow lay heavy on the slopes, people, as they always had done, turned up again to skate and to enjoy sledging, sliding, snowballing and all the simple pleasures afforded by a keen white winter.

The Cartwright Hall added to the post-war revival of the Park as a whole, holding first a major exhibition marking out future plans and hopes for the city. Textiles, engineering and art were all represented, together with a large architect's model of Bradford's centre. This portrayed a completely re-designed Forster Square overlooked by the Cathedral no longer to be hidden behind the General Post Office building, which it was proposed should be demolished.

In more recent years there has been a period of dramatic change. On a walk through the Park today you will no longer find the old boathouse, the Masham Cafe, the greenhouses and conservatory, the lido swimming pool, the bandstands, or even the children's paddling pool. All have gone. Only the Cartwright Memorial Hall stands

Figure 14. Cartwright Hall, 2000. *Peter Shutt.*

changeless before its forecourt of flowers. However, brighter times are now once more beckoning. The colourful delights of the Mela and ever changing exhibitions in the Cartwright, have all brought life back into the Park. (Figure 14)

With the help of the Lottery Heritage Fund the Park is now undergoing a genuine revival. A new boat-house has already been built, the lake cleaned and the lake edge walk provided with new decorative cast iron seats at strategic intervals.

Once a gentleman's private estate, now a much loved public Park, it has been enjoyed by generations of Bradfordians for over a hundred years. The future looks bright.

I think Samuel Cunliffe Lister would have been well pleased.

9. H.L.B.L. AND THE FOUNTAIN BREWERY

by Anthony Avis

I BEGAN THESE NOTES ABOUT MY ASSOCIATION with Hammond's brewery in 1956. I was resident in Bradford and had a room in a private hotel in Manningham Lane. It was a comfortable lodging house, and there were a dozen lodgers. We were provided with breakfast and dinner, had a common sitting-room and separate bedrooms. All of us were young and at the beginning of our careers; there were ten young men and two young women. Of the men, eight were connected with the woollen trade, from dealing with raw wool straight off the backs of colonial sheep, through scouring, spinning, weaving and dyeing, to selling the finished bolts of cloth - which shows the dominance of that industry then in Bradford. Moreover, three of the eight men were from the commonwealth countries of Australia, Canada and South Africa, and were over in the old country to learn the trade and maintain the contacts. All raw wool still came to Bradford Wool Exchange to be auctioned and the Conditioning House still appraised its quality and issued its certificates. Soon it would all change and the old colonial producers of raw materials would do these jobs themselves in their own countries and their young men would cease to come over.

As for the two girls, they, and one of the young men, were employed by the newly rising mail order firms based in the city. The girls were considered unusual for the times - single, away from home, independent - the first of the rising contingent of female executives; although the word 'executive' had still to be imported from the USA to describe that growing class of employees of a large company. And there was I, the secretary of a brewery company, much to be

Figure 1. Part of the transport fleet of Hammond's United Breweries Ltd. *City of Bradford Official Handbook, 1961.*

admired, having the ready and welcome entry to the city's hostelries, and his name on the sides of the Post Office red brewery delivery wagons trundling round the Bradford streets. It was on one of the cab doors: 'A. Avis, Company Secretary, Hammond's United Breweries Ltd' (Figure 1). All the companies which had a transport fleet displayed this information; why I do not know - perhaps it was the law of the land then to do so. Anyway, it gave me a sense of unaccustomed importance and it impressed my fellow lodgers.

There was little or no hanky panky in our lodging house; first, because the manners and the traditions were against loose relationships, and secondly our landlady kept an eagle eye and a sharp ear on all movements in the house. We were, by today's relaxed standards, remarkably innocent and well behaved. Television was not a great attraction to pass away the idle hours; in the evenings, after dinner, we tended to sit around in the lounge and talk, read the papers, and then go out for a drink in the *Spotted House* or the *Turf* pubs nearby, and return to our rooms, and bed. Most of us had varying kinds of homework to do, whether study or bringing tasks back from the office. In this scheme of things I hatched my idea of writing down an account of how I came to be in Bradford, in a small cold bedroom, on a winter's night, with little more than the periodic whirr of the electric trolleybus as it stopped and started at the bus stop below my window. It was 1956; there were very few private cars on the roads, and not many people went back into the city centre at night-time, and those who did, went on the trolleybus. So Manningham Lane was like a quiet suburban street and I could write down my thoughts in solitude.

I wrote when I could, and often there would be many weeks between my efforts and I would lose the continuity of my narrative. However, I plunged on and found I was as interested in describing people, their habits and customs, as I was of setting down my life story. I finally came to a conclusion and read through my work and found I had written a limited social history of the 1950s in a northern provincial city with the directors and employees of a brewery as the main characters - *primus inter pares* was Harry Lawrence Bradfer-Lawrence (H.L.B.L.), the chairman and inspiration of the company (Figure 2).

Figure 2. Harry Lawrence Bradfer-Lawrence (H.L.B.L.) in 1957. *The Brewers' Society.*

Figure 3. Hammond's *Fountain Inn*, Manchester Road, in the 1950s. *Bradford Libraries.*

Hammond's Bradford Brewery Company Limited, which had its headquarters at Fountain Brewery, was H.L.B.L's seat of power in Yorkshire (Figures 3 and 4). By good fortune he gained control of it in 1937, having come to the county as land agent for a branch of the Aykroyd family, long established in all divisions of the Bradford wool

Figure 4. Entrance to the Fountain Brewery under the crouching lions. *Malcolm Toft.*

Figure 5. Ezra Waugh Hammond, of Hammond's Brewery, as Mayor of Bradford, 1890-91. *Malcolm Toft.*

trade. This branch, led by Sir William Henry Aykroyd, had a large estate of some six thousand acres, at Grantley, near Ripon, and in 1934 he was looking for someone to administer it and through the informal network of communication in these matters, he learned that H.L.B.L. was available for consideration. Sir William's wife (Emma Louisa), whom he married in 1890, was the daughter of Ezra Waugh Hammond, the eponymous owner of the brewery, and on his death she inherited a shareholding in the company (Figure 5). So Sir William, by marriage, found himself chairman of a concern in which he had no expertise or interest.[1] Its faltering prosperity in the 1930s irritated him and he was relieved to learn that H.L.B.L. had experience of managing a brewery estate, from his connections with the Bagge family of King's Lynn, Norfolk, who had also owned a brewery amongst its commercial enterprises. Swiftly he offered him the job of running it and by 1935 he was joint managing director with Fred Wilkins (Managing Director since 1912), and two years later managing director. He became chairman in 1943. He soon restored the company's fortunes, helped by the onset of war. Sir William retired

Figure 6. Hammond's Fountain Brewery advertisement. *Malcolm Toft.*

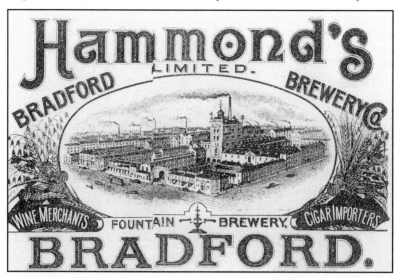

Figure 7. The site of the Fountain Brewery surrounded by factories, mills, shops and terraced houses. *Wood Visual Communications.*

from the company in 1943 and was succeeded by his son, Sir Alfred, as a non-executive director. From 1937 to 1960 H.L.B.L. had complete control and expanded its profits, its assets and its standing in the brewery world.

Until 1955, when it ceased brewing, the business was a complete brewery operation - it brewed and bottled beer; it had a large wines, spirits and tobacco business, a mineral water factory, its own maltings, a tied estate which was spreading across northern England; and all the ancillary trades associated with a brewery company (Figure 6). The site of its activity was two acres of land adjoining Manchester Road, a half mile from the city centre and among the nineteenth century development of factories, mills, shops and terraced houses (Figure 7). From the late 1950s it became increasingly clear that the Victorian industrial development had run its course, that the land needed to be cleared and a fresh start made. Within twenty years this happened, and today nothing remains of Fountain Brewery to indicate where once it had stood and flourished.

In the 1950s, from the city centre as far as Rooley Lane on both sides of Manchester Road, there was an almost unbroken succession of shops, for this road was the main shopping street for the majority of Bradford citizens, where they bought the necessities of life from shopkeepers and tradesmen who lived over their premises. Their customers came from a great hinterland of row upon row of stone terraced housing, mostly back-to-back for economy of construction, who worked in the mills, foundries, workshops, warehouses and factories scattered about the area. Manchester Road, on Saturday afternoon and early evening, was a splendid scene of crowds of shoppers, and the display of foodstuffs and goods of all kinds inside and outside the shops, with all the bustle and the stir of humanity. And then there were the crowds of men making their way up to Odsal Stadium to watch Bradford Northern in a rugby league game.

Just about every shop was personally owned and run by the occupier, and in the years I worked at the brewery I came to know many of them. In fact, Hammond's owned a parade of small shops as part of the brewery estate, which I administered, and I employed Sam Chippindale to collect the rents in those days before he went into town centre property development on a large scale and became one of the country's leading figures in this field in partnership with his friend Arnold Hagenbach, a Wakefield baker (Figure 8).

The rise of the grocery supermarket wiped away the independent shops, and soon the popularity of motor car ownership led to the building of huge shopping complexes on the outskirts of towns and

Figure 8. Hammond's Fountain Brewery Office and the *Fountain Inn,* Manchester Road. *Bradford Libraries.*

cities to accommodate it. The old life and culture, which was Manchester Road, vanished. There, in the 1950s, on a Saturday afternoon (remember people still worked on Saturday mornings then), you went in and out of one shop after another to buy your food needs, from the butcher to the baker, and then the greengrocer, the fishmonger and so on. Perhaps it was a tiresome business; you shopped for the week's needs and carried away what you bought. If you were better class and you had an account, the tradesman would deliver for you on the following Monday. It was a drawn-out chore, but it had its vitality in human communication; you exchanged greetings and insults with people you knew, and stopped to exchange the time of day. You were part of a crowd for whom Saturday shopping was a ritual occasion, and not one to be hurried through with impatience.

In the road were the tram tracks. The trams rattled along in the middle of the road, swaying from side to side, and if you were one of the few persons to be driving a car, you were very careful not to get your front wheels stuck in the rails or to skid on them in wet weather. The wool trade was supreme in the city then, with enormous motor wagons grinding up the road loaded with bales of wool and belching black smoke like railway engines, and fit to suffocate you if you were following. There were still significant numbers of horses and carts hauling wool about, whose drivers saw no need to indicate where they were going. The cautious pedestrian stuck to the pavement for safety and hygienic reasons. I am sure I remember Manchester Road, in part at least, was still cobbled in 1948, as I have an impression of watching horses slipping and sliding to get a grip when pulling uphill. There were still water troughs in the streets to slake the thirst of the passing labouring horses.

As for the streets behind Manchester Road and their warren-like complexity, if you wanted to take a short cut across to Saint Luke's Hospital in Little Horton Lane you had to have local knowledge to find your way. In wintertime a piercing wind swept down from Odsal Top like a scythe, cutting through the heaviest worsted overcoat; you were glad to turn the corner for relief. In summertime when there was no wind, the pall of chimney smoke from every factory, mill and cottage hung over the city and obscured the sun and the inhabitants coughed and spluttered and sucked locally made throat lozenges as if they were sweets. Every building was made of stone, the walls and the roofs impregnated with the smoke and dirt of generations; the prevailing colours were shades of black, grey and brown.

The brewery site had originally been developed as a malting in 1830. It became a brewery a decade later and steadily expanded its

Figure 9. The tower of Fountain Brewery dominates. *Malcolm Toft.*

activities through the nineteenth century. By the start of the next century it had within its boundaries, as I have previously mentioned, all the commercial and practical trades associated with a lively and substantial business. This was the position when I first knew it. I had the impression of people tumbling over one another on a cramped site (Figure 9); and it was a valid impression, for H.L.B.L. began his expansion programme in 1944 by buying Bentley & Shaw of Huddersfield for its extensive brewery estate, followed by Tadcaster Tower Brewery of York for the same reason. Thereafter Fountain Brewery by degrees became just an administration centre. It was a wise move on his part, for he anticipated and dealt with the looming problems that Bradford presented.

In 1964 the significant administration was moved to York and Bradford became just a local office; even this activity ceased in January 1968 and the site was sold to Bradford Corporation.

It was agreed that I should report at Fountain Brewery on 1 January 1956 to begin my duties. On that day I took a train to Bradford, accompanied by two well filled suitcases, and eventually arrived at Exchange station. It was snowing. I went on to the forecourt, hailed a taxi and asked the driver where I could find some lodgings. He took me to a boarding house in Manningham Lane, where I acquired a room and having enquired how to get to the brewery, caught a trolley bus into the city centre and walked up Manchester Road. I arrived at about 4.00pm and began my first day with Hammond's United Breweries Ltd. New Year's Day was not strictly observed then as a public holiday; the brewery offices were sort of half open and half closed, but H.L.B.L's secretary was there, totally embarrassed by my appearance and what to do with me until the office closed at 5.30pm. Priggishly, I had made my point - that when I said I would report for duty on 1 January, I had in fact done so. I wandered about and opened doors and introduced myself to startled senior employees and their clerks. I then walked all the way back to the boarding house in the slush.

In the ensuing months I came to know all who worked in Fountain Brewery, and at the outlying offices at Huddersfield, Tadcaster, York, Scunthorpe, Darlington and Newcastle upon Tyne. My job encompassed being company secretary, estates and legal manager, secretary to the management committee (H.L.B.L. and P.L.B.L., his son Colonel Philip Bradfer-Lawrence, in conclave), secretary to the pension scheme, and compiler of trade statistics. Combined, these posts were pivotal in the company: I was the conduit by which all matters flowed to the chairman and managing director, and by which many of the decisions flowed out. I knew what they thought about all senior employees and their abilities. My personal relationship with H.L.B.L. was of enormous significance and consequence as he had no confidant within the company. I found that I was being sent for to attend in his office to discuss legal and semi-legal matters which he expanded into sessions of thinking aloud his inmost thoughts and inviting my suggestions (Figure 10). At first I could offer little advice, as I knew the business little enough, but time helped in dealing with this, plus my own extensive travels through the widespread company. P.L.B.L. soon appreciated this and it helped our business relationship, particularly as he began to realise that he could

Figure 10. Mr Bradfer-Lawrence's desk. *Malcolm Toft.*

sometimes get his own plans approved by H.L.B.L. if they were discussed with me beforehand. It was an astonishing position of influence in which I found myself, achieved within a very short space of time. Curiously, I never really appreciated that position; office politics then in the medium sized companies did not exist, loyalty and long service were still the abiding virtues. My instinct and professional training kept my ears open and my mouth shut. I cannot possibly assert that I became, within a few months of employment by Hammond's, a person of importance in the company. It was not so, and the senior employees with long service continued to exercise their influence. But as the months passed the special and unusual circumstances which applied in my case took hold and, supported by my legal training and ability to offer disinterested advice, lifted me to a powerful position.

After a year H.L.B.L. and P.L.B.L. agreed I should act as secretary to a management committee of the two of them, gathering up matters referred to them and to myself from senior employees and requiring a direction, to replace the haphazard and piecemeal approaches to one or other of them. It met once a month. I prepared an agenda, with supporting papers, added as necessary any subsidiary background, recorded their decisions and circulated them. It was a relief for PLBL, as those decisions were set out in approved minutes; H.L.B.L. in the past had shown a tendency to deny or alter rulings he had given, which placed P.L.B.L. in a very difficult position.

There had never been regular contact between H.L.B.L. and senior employees. They were sent for as needed when he was considering a problem involving them, and they would leave whatever they were doing and literally run to his office when he would launch into detail on some matter he had been considering for some time. The result was that those employees were often ill-prepared for the encounter, incoherent, and then were thought to be fools and incompetent. P.L.B.L. could see this situation clearly and endeavoured to bring in a rational system of consultation and communication, which did not appeal to father.

He therefore saw my appearance as his chance to set up the committee of management with myself as secretary. It was done and I soon saw the advantages and the pitfalls. It took some time for H.L.B.L. to accept that written minutes approved and signed by him were essential, that they could not be ignored and his own recollection of what had been agreed substituted. So I had three years of fairly nerve-racking meetings, getting agreement on the minutes, getting them signed, and implementing the decisions. It was

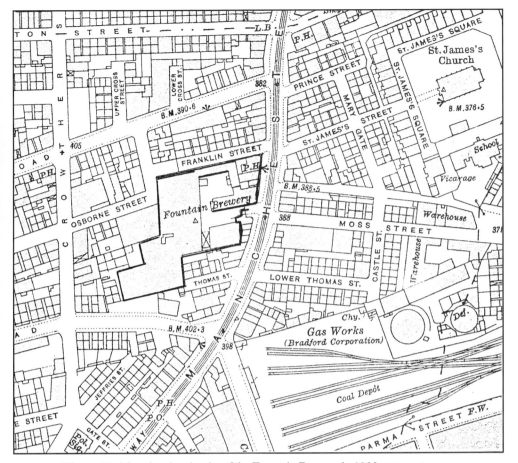

Figure 11. Map showing the site of the Fountain Brewery in 1933. *Ordnance Survey.*

enjoyable though, and taught me much about men and manners. I found myself able to predict quite accurately the attitudes of those involved and what they would do, and could therefore offer appropriate advice to H.L.B.L. and P.L.B.L. accordingly. This raised my esteem with them when I offered advice and views about what would be likely to happen, and which did in fact happen; and that I could use the abilities of senior employees.

After two years I was made secretary of the company and came into close contact with the non executive directors, most of whom were descendants of the original founders of the various companies and who held their appointments by virtue of large shareholdings, and some sentiment. They were all amiable and pleasant men, fascinated by the expertise of H.L.B.L. and his ability to turn their once very ordinary shares in sleepy companies into possessions of increasing value. They did not know quite what to make of him, had their misgivings and heard the gossip, but were too polite or discreet to voice their thoughts aloud. All of them were well off because of inherited money and the Hammond's shares which gave them their place on the board. H.L.B.L. doubled, and doubled again, the value of those shareholdings, and bestowed on them as directors a reflected power through his success. Only one outside director, Edward Thompson, really understood the workings of the company and was in a position to ask searching questions of H.L.B.L. at board meetings. He was the chairman himself of a brewery company much larger than Hammond's (Ind Coope & Allsopp Ltd.) and a hoped-for friend if ever there was to be a time of need. He never used his position to embarrass though, and H.L.B.L. ran the meetings and the company as a one man show.

Once a month the board of directors would meet at Bradford, travelling there from their various country estates around the north of England, ready to begin at promptly eleven o'clock. They would arrive and their cars would be lined up in the yard at Fountain Brewery, (Figure 12) indicating to the office staff who looked out of their windows that it was indeed board meeting day. It invested that day in each month with particular significance, and the presence of the motor cars was a visible and physical manifestation evidence that the lists of figures and the reports demanded by H.L.B.L., and prepared by the departmental heads with much anxiety, were now to be made. The directors assembled in the first floor boardroom, with its enormous table, the dignified Chippendale chairs down either side, a huge high backed armchair for the chairman, and a slightly smaller one at the other end for the deputy chairman. In each corner of the room were small pieces of furniture, all antique, and some of such venerable decrepitude that leaning against them or putting a hand on them stood every chance of loosening a strip of veneer or beading. The boardroom received its natural light from a row of windows on one side and from a venerable and distinguished chandelier which cast much lustre and rather less illumination. The walls were filled with a very large glass fronted bookcase filled with ancient tooled leather volumes, never looked at but looking very learned on the shelves, and oil paintings of English and Dutch landscape scenes, which also were never looked at. The style was patrician, the atmosphere one of continuing tradition.

The Hammond's board meetings would end just before 1 pm and it was my duty to ensure that a fleet of cars was waiting at the front door to transport the directors to the *Alexandra Hotel*, owned by the company and in the city centre across the road from the Alhambra Theatre. Since I was never certain when the board meeting would exactly finish, and since I had no electronic means, as exist today, to inform the outside world of its conclusion, I had a problem on my hands. I solved it by arranging with the transport manager that he would maintain watch on the boardroom windows around 1pm and he would see me wave a paper and this would be the signal to bring the cars to the front door. Miraculously the simple ploy worked very well - as well as any white smoke from a Vatican chimney. The previous secretary had constant trouble with H.L.B.L., as the cars were never at the door in time. H.L.B.L. was annoyed by having to wait even a few minutes, particularly in the doorway of his own brewery and in the public gaze. I suppose this small manoeuvre did as much as anything to impress H.L.B.L. of my efficiency; on such slight gestures are reputations built.

The chairman would graciously invite the vice-chairman, and whoever happened to be in favour among the directors, to accompany him in his Bentley car, which led the cavalcade down Manchester Road. Into the succeeding cars the remaining members and myself tumbled as best we could and away we went down into Town Hall Square, with the policeman on duty knowing who we were, and holding up the traffic to let us sweep through and up Great Horton Road and into the hotel entrance. The chairman would hasten out, so far as his gammy leg permitted, without always waiting for the chauffeur to open the door, and lead the way to the first floor private dining-room, with its notice board 'Directors Dining-Room' to impress the ignorant. I was last in rather like the sheepdog behind

Figure 12. The *Alexandra Hotel*, Great Norton Road. *Illustrated Weekly Telegraph.*

the flock and the hotel manager always asked in a whisper if 'he' was in a good mood. Most of the time I could confirm he was, because H.L.B.L. had to watch himself in front of the other directors, if only to preserve the carefully constructed facade of well-bred behaviour. Sometimes, instead of a drink at the brewery, we used to have pre lunch drinks in an annexe to the dining-room and H.L.B.L. would carry on his usual kind of talk to which the others found it very difficult to respond. After a couple of drinks, and with the high level of artificial bonhomie sustained, the chairman would proceed into the dining-room. He would elaborately arrange the placings, the vice-chairman ostentatiously offered the end seat, and he would pick those to sit on his right and left. He always ate his food extremely quickly, and was not a big eater anyway, with the result that slow eaters would be embarrassed, when looking up from their plates, to see he was finished and looking around with some impatience.

The luncheons always ended promptly, with the chairman consulting his blind man's hunter watch with some ostentation and announcing that he had to leave on non-specified but important business, which occasioned yet more dyspepsia. Seated at the end of the table and near to the door, it was my signal unobtrusively to scuttle out and summon the cars to the hotel entrance, and organise the return to the brewery. The cavalcade of cars swept back in the same imperious manner they had come, the policeman on point duty held up the traffic and the brewery yardmen watched from the safety of the old boilerhouse doors. Farewells were made and the chairman continued his elaborate conversation accompanied by the issue of kind regards to distant wives and relatives; and it was all over for another month.

A paragraph on the menus for these luncheons. They had to be approved by the chairman as he still recalled with horror at the early days, when the food produced displayed gastronomic ignorance and a fair resemblance to what could be obtained from one of the food stalls in Kirkgate Market. I soon gathered what he considered proper, which was that the starter and the pudding could have exotic touches but the main course had to be traditional English cooking, and he left it to me thereafter. He liked a foreign sounding soup or pâté to start with, a traditional meat course, a reasonably elaborate pudding, and a half Stilton cheese, port fed. The wines were always good, sent over from Huddersfield by Tim Westerby, the company wine and spirit manager, a man of great experience and discernment. Curiously, none of the company's beer was ever produced. I rather think some of the more distant directors had never sampled our beer.

To return to Fountain Brewery. On the creation of United Breweries[2] in 1960 Hammond's ceased to exist as an independent company, and the centre of activity moved from Bradford to York. Fountain Brewery immediately went into decline, and this coincided with the declining years and importance of H.L.B.L., by now seventy-five years old. The seat of government became fixed at York and it was obvious to all who worked at Fountain Brewery that ultimate authority resided in York also. Routine functions were still carried on at Bradford, particularly accounting, so a temporary air of busyness still pervaded the offices there, but the writing was on the wall, clear for all to see. Brewing had ceased in 1954, leaving the brewing tower empty; then followed the closure of the bottling facilities, and the steady removal of all the commercial activities and warehousing. The only buildings in full occupation remained the offices. Bradford Corporation for some years past had been proceeding with slum clearance programmes in the hinterland of streets of terraced housing, and many rows of good houses were pulled down simply because they were back-to-back and deemed unhealthy. This left the brewery estate standing like a dilapidated fortress in a wasteland. United Breweries merged with Charrington of London in 1963 and the head office moved to London. In the following year it was decided that the new and empty York offices should become the headquarters of the northern division of Charrington United Breweries. Fountain Brewery closed and was taken over by the corporation and demolished. Today nothing exists to show where once it stood, an urban motorway passes over its site. H.L.B.L. lived long enough to see Fountain Brewery close and be sold. He died before it was demolished. He, like the brewery he had built up, had mellowed with age and in his last years he was held in great affection for his charm, his waywardness, his manner of speech and the evocation of happy times - curious, really, but distance tends to add enchantment to the view.

These are my recollections written a decade since Hammond's vanished from the brewery scene. For me Fountain Brewery is inextricably mixed up with my memories of H.L.B.L.. In its one hundred and thirty years the brewery undoubtedly had other men of great character associated with it, notably James and Ezra Waugh Hammond, father and son; but all I know of them is from what I have read, and from gazing at their stiff Victorian photographs. H.L.B.L. I knew in the flesh, complete with his mannerisms, his likes and dislikes. He dominated our working lives and appeared before us suddenly in the ramshackle office corridors. We knew when he was in the brewery by instinct; the employees were sufficiently few in number for him to know almost everybody. Middle management was small and orders came from him with little intervention and the results of everybody's labours were as directly known to him. We felt extraordinarily pleased if he approved what we were doing, and very downcast if he did not. We felt baffled and angered if the fancy took him to ignore his previous instructions and left us adrift, or if he disapproved of some action by us of which we felt quite proud, only to find it was not his view and that he sharply said so.

On reflection, we seemed to live and work in a much more intensely personal atmosphere than now prevails in the larger commercial organisations: highly formalised, stratified and depersonalised. No doubt they achieve on a much greater scale and seemingly in a planned and logical way, but there is no feeling of working for someone who is blood and flesh and whom we are anxious to please. We did not consider then that we were really working for a company - or rather that we were, but it was H.L.B.L. who was the company. We had no doubt either where our duty lay - it was to him, and if we pleased our tenants, our managers and our free trade customers, the shareholders and the general public on the streets of Bradford as well, we were mildly surprised and that much more satisfied. I suppose it was something to have the object of one's endeavours so readily identified.

Notes and References

1 Hammond's, a limited company, was formed in 1889, but experienced financial problems 1892-94. A new board of directors was formed in 1894, with Sir William Aykroyd a director and Edward Dobson chairman. Dobson died in 1912 when Sir William became chairman and Fred Wilkins managing director. The company was successful until the effects of the depression. In 1930 dividends were 10 per cent, 1931 - 6 per cent, none in 1932, 1933 and 1934, 1935 - 2 $^{1}/_{2}$ per cent, 1936 - 5 per cent, 1937 - 8 per cent, 1938 - 8 per cent, 1939 - 8 per cent, 1940 - 8 per cent. In 1935, Hammond's had some 250 public houses and a weekly barrelage of approximately 500.
2 United Breweries was formed by a merger of Hammond's United Breweries, Hope & Anchor Breweries Ltd, Sheffield, and John Jeffrey & Co. Ltd of Edinburgh. The force behind the new holding company was the Canadian, Edward Taylor, with his Carling Black Label lager as its flagship brand. At the time of the 1960 merger, Hammond's United Brewery had over 1,200 public houses and a weekly barrelage of approximately 8,000.

I am indebted to Malcolm Toft for these notes, and the supply of illustrations. Editor.

10. A Patient's Lot at the Westgate Infirmary

by Christine Alvin

BRADFORD INFIRMARY WAS SET UP as a charitable hospital in 1825 to treat the 'indigent poor' of the town. In 1843 a new building in the Tudor style - 'the finest structure in Bradford' - was opened as the new infirmary on the junction of Westgate and Lumb Lane (Figure 1). By 1909 Bradford's expanding population had

Figure 1. The Bradford Infirmary. *Bradford Libraries..*

rendered it, and its later extensions, inadequate, and the Lord Mayor, Sir James Hill, started a public appeal for a new building. The First World War and the subsequent slump delayed matters, and the new infirmary - the Bradford Royal Infirmary - on Duckworth Lane was not completed until 1936 when the last patients left Westgate.

To obtain treatment, the sick, known as 'proper objects', had to find a subscriber or donor to the Infirmary who would give them a recommendation to attend the Infirmary. Most of the Infirmary's work was with out-patients and with home-patients who were visited at their homes, as patients of general practitioners are now. Lack of money meant that the number of in-patients grew slowly; there were only 220 beds by the end of the nineteenth century. In 1900 over 2,000 in-patients were treated, 7,000 out-patients, over 2,500 home-patients, and over 3,000 casualties. The staff included five resident doctors, forty-seven nurses and probationers, and ten honorary consultants attending twice a week (Figure 2).

Figure 2. Outpatients' waiting room. *Bradford Infirmary Report, 1913.*

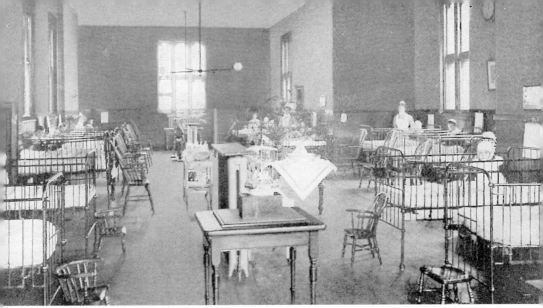

Figure 3. Children's surgical ward. *Bradford Infirmary Report, 1913.*

The Patients

The patients were mostly low-paid unskilled workers. Those who were betteroff were expected to pay for treatment, including surgery in their own homes, by general practitioners. Paupers were treated either by doctors employed by the Board of Guardians, or in the Workhouse Infirmary.

Not all the 'indigent poor' were accepted as patients in charitable hospitals. Most had rules excluding certain groups, but only paupers were specifically excluded from the Bradford Infirmary. However, children were rarely admitted until a ward was dedicated for their use after the Infirmary was extended in 1863 (Figure 3). Until then there were only 'children's cots distributed about the women's wards'. Before the establishment of a separate Fever Hospital in 1871, patients with fevers were only reluctantly admitted because of the danger of infection; thus 'an occasional case under a special nurse and in one of the small wards' might be accepted. Venereal diseases were treated at the Infirmary, although many hospitals barred them. A *Pharmacopœia* printed for the Infirmary in 1878 had several remedies for such complaints. Most cases were treated as out-patients, but some were in-patients. In 1877 the House Committee discussed the case of a syphilitic girl of five who was an in-patient. She was 'an orphan and has contracted primary syphilis in the filthy den from which she was brought', but was removed to the workhouse 'to avoid further contamination'. In 1881 the medical staff called for new facilities to include separate 'foul' wards for patients with venereal diseases. Midwifery cases were not admitted, although after the appointment of a gynaecologist in 1891, women suffering from post-natal complications were admitted.

There are few early records showing the diseases suffered by Infirmary patients, but a Medical Officer of the Infirmary compiled a list of the disorders suffered by mill hands attending as out-patients during 1859. There were 828 cases, amongst which phthisis or tuberculosis predominated, with 114 cases, and scrofula or tuberculosis of the glands followed with ninety-six cases. Sufferers from dyspepsia, uterine diseases, syphilis and debility made up many of the remaining cases. 1863 was the first year in which detailed statistics of patient cases were produced. This showed a wide range of diseases treated, seventy-nine operations performed, and a large number of accident cases.

Although hospitals with a high proportion of accident cases could expect a high death-rate from operations, the rate in Bradford was average, and it was said by the resident officers of the hospital that most of the accident patients were 'working people in good health, well nourished, and of tolerably sober habits', and that a 'liberal allowance of support and stimulants' contributed to their recovery. Many, but not all, accidents were work related. Thus, during one week, accident cases admitted included crushed feet from an accident at work and from a fall into a cellar, a fractured leg from a riding accident, and a cut leg from an accident on a glass roof. On another occasion when deaths in the Infirmary were reported in the *Bradford Observer* they included two infant deaths from scalding and one from burning, and a case of accidental poisoning.

Patient Rules and Behaviour

Patients were admitted on one day a week until later in the century when daily admissions began. Once admitted, patients faced a formidable list of rules governing their behaviour. Strict obedience to the House Surgeon and Matron was required, and the patient 'shall do such work as they [the House Surgeon or Matron] shall appoint under the direction of the Physician or Surgeon'. Patients were allowed out to visit church on Sunday, but nowhere else without permission, nor into other wards. Anyone

> *wilfully neglecting any of these Rules, or on account of any other irregularity, shall not partake of the benefits of the Charity again.*

Swearing, behaving rudely or indecently, and smoking were later added to the list of offences, and the work to be done by patients was defined to include assistance with nursing other patients. Cases were recorded of patients being dismissed for infringing the rules. In 1851,

Ellen Henry was brought before the Board. She has been in the habit of saving her food and giving it to her sister who has been found with bread and meat in the Dirty Linen she was taking away.

Another patient was refused admission 'in consequence of bad conduct and irregularity when an in-patient some time ago'. Patients had to provide sufficient of their own linen for their stay in hospital, which even by the end of the century still averaged twenty-seven days. This was difficult for some patients, and the Ladies Committee, who looked after the welfare of patients, provided supplies of shirts, bedgowns, chemises and nightcaps. Slippers were provided by the Infirmary by the 1850s, but were 'frequently missed' when patients left. No doubt the rule requiring patients to supply their own knife, fork, spoon, soap and towel also caused problems for the poorer patients.

Rules for visitors were equally stringent. Initially they were allowed to visit only one day a week. This was increased to two days, but later reduced to one day because,

...it will be far better for the patients, it will be a great relief to the Nurses and servants, and will much increase the cleanliness of the Institution.

By 1900 the visiting hour was on two days a week. Visitors were 'required to come clean and tidily dressed' or they would be refused

Figure 4. Male surgical ward. *Bradford Infirmary Report, 1914.*

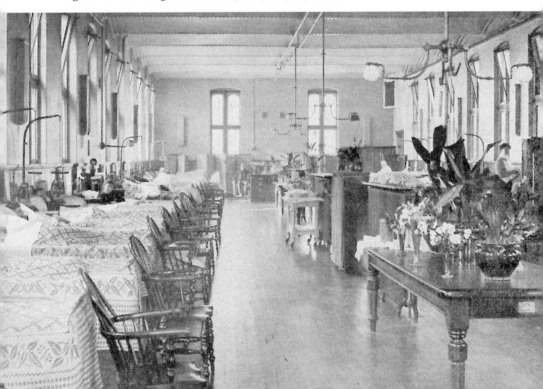

admission, and were not allowed to sit on the beds (Figure 4). Complaints about their behaviour led to copies of the rules being printed and handed out to friends of in-patients on admission. In 1825 a rule was made forbidding visitors to bring food or drink for patients. This was later reinforced until it included 'sweetmeats, fruits, liquids, or eatables of any kind or description'. Staff made searches of lockers after visiting times to confiscate food and drink. In 1892 it was reported that,

> *... a medical gentleman went the round of the lockers in one ward, and filled two large trays with edibles of various descriptions, including short-cakes, spice-cakes, biscuits, nuts, and oranges, while it was found that one visitor had intended to regale a patient with pork pies and liquors.*

The possible consequences of breaking the rule were shown in an inquest report on a patient who died after surreptitiously drinking brandy smuggled in by his wife. Evidently visitors broke other rules, especially those limiting their numbers. A house surgeon remarked at another inquest, 'nothing did more to hinder the recovery of a patient than the presence of friends', although in that case it was the parents of a dying boy who had been refused permission to visit him, which suggests that the rules, although necessary, could have been applied less rigorously.

Hospital Conditions

In 1850 the Weekly Committee first referred to the need for 'providing convenience for washing in each ward, and a night commode for each ward' and a bill was paid for baths the following year, but there is little evidence that washing and sanitary facilities for patients were given a high priority. In 1873 it was decided that 'a fire should be lighted in each bath room on Tuesday mornings during the cold weather', which suggests that there was little encouragement for patients to keep themselves clean. A report in 1892 described the older part of the hospital as 'having only one bath, although it contains four good-sized wards, in addition to smaller ones' on each floor. The larger wards, containing twenty-one beds,

> *...have no lavatory or 'slop sink' in any proper meaning of that term. In the middle of each ward there are two doors which open into two cupboards, one of which contains a water closet and tap for cold water, and the other two or three wash basins. Such a state of affairs is not defensible, as the hospital authorities admit.*

Figure 5. Laundry, Bradford Infirmary, c1930. *Bradford Libraries.*

In the newer part of the Infirmary, however, 'the fittings, bath, and lavatory accommodation reflect great credit upon the authorities'. Improvements in standards of cleanliness, both in and out of the hospital, relieved the Infirmary of problems with 'vermin' which had caused wards to be closed, and nurses to be told to 'examine and report on the state of the Bedding and Mattresses used by one patient before the bed is occupied by another'. Indeed, a visitor in 1867 commented on the 'soft beds, with linen clean and soft as snow' (Figure 5).

Offensive smells permeated the hospital from the Dead Room or mortuary, from the recurrently defective drains, or because of the condition of particular patients. The Ladies Committee commented on 'the offensive smell arising from the poor woman in Ward number 1, who is suffering from severe burns' and made a compassionate plea that such patients should be placed in one of the smaller wards, as, 'they think the health of the other patients must be prejudicially affected by being in the same ward as such cases'. Bad ventilation and overcrowding in the original parts of the 1843 Infirmary building meant that 'the hospital odour was very pervasive'. The odour sometimes heralded an outbreak of the dreaded infectious 'hospital diseases' rife in nineteenth century hospitals, such as pyemia, a serious and sometimes fatal form of blood poisoning, which broke out in the Infirmary in 1870. Patients had to be housed outside in tents, which blew down one night in a gale, or sent to hospital in Ilkley. Wards were fumigated, whitewashed, and re-fumigated before they could be used again. In 1879 an outbreak of erysipelas, another

Figure 6. A Named Bed. *Bradford Royal Infirmary: an epitome, 1912.*

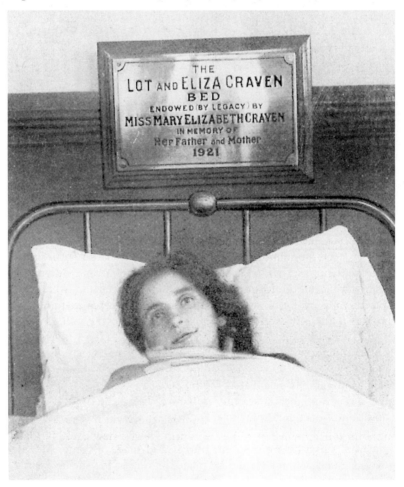

equally severe infection, resulted in the complete refurbishment of wards, their furnishings, sanitation and drainage. The spread of antiseptic procedures and an increased emphasis on cleanliness led to the decline of such outbreaks.

Whilst efforts were being made to improve hospital hygiene, the patients' welfare was also being improved by the efforts of the governors and charitable donors to provide them with books and occupations of an appropriate nature. A guinea was allocated to be spent on books for patients in 1847, but those supplied by visitors were to be shown by the Matron to the Weekly Committee, after novels were introduced among the patients. Thereafter suitable books, newspapers and other gifts became a common method of helping the Infirmary patients. Flowers were also donated, and pictures for the walls. A harmonium was given to the children's ward, and toys, although these were later criticised as being too limited, and the harmonium as being unused through lack of competent musicians. The Ladies Committee visited the wards every week, enquiring into the patients' wellbeing, reading to those who wished it, 'to alleviate the tedium of the long, and to many of the patients, suffering hours of the day,' and accepting the thanks of the grateful patients for 'the kind attention shown them by the doctors and nurses'.

Hospital Food

If the patients' visitors brought food for them it was perhaps to relieve the monotony of the hospital diet. Diet tables for male patients in 1863 show that unlimited quantities of bread, potatoes, and butter were allowed, with a pint each of gruel, soup and milk each day, and 6oz of meat on alternate days. By 1900 the diet was still monotonous and stolid, but the quantities were less. Dinner consisted of 4oz of meat, 8oz of potatoes, 2oz of bread and 4oz of rice pudding. Breakfast and tea were meals of 'sufficient bread and butter' and a pint of tea, and supper was half a pint of milk or gruel. Patients may have been grateful for the variety added by official gifts from donors of grapes, oranges and other fruit. Such gifts were acceptable, unlike the smuggled gifts of visitors.

The quality of the food was variable. The Ladies Committee regularly received complaints about the quality of the bread and meat, and made suggestions to improve the variety of meals. They noted improvements after the appointment of a new cook, but later suggested that,

In view of the frequent troubles in the kitchen through the intemperance of the Different Cooks the Ladies wish to suggest that an allowance of Tea, Coffee or Milk be given to the servants instead of Beer.

However, by 1892 the diet and food were judged satisfactory, and the bread, baked on the premises, was highly praised.

Medicine and Surgery

Little can be found in the various Minute Books of the Infirmary about the medical and surgical treatment of patients. The earliest reference to medical treatment was in 1828, when it was decided that 'Ann Eltoft of Cannon Street be appointed to apply leeches for the Dispensary'. By this date leeches were used less as a means of bloodletting than to relieve inflammation, and suitable leeches were rare and becoming expensive. The Infirmary continued to use them at least until the 1860s, when an average quarterly account showed that they cost over £12.

A few items were frequently mentioned in the Minute Books. In 1841 the Weekly Board ordered that 'in future the poultices be made from linseed meal instead of bread', and thereafter large quantities of linseed were ordered; in 1858 the amount was 10 cwt at a time. It was used in hot poultices in cases of inflammation, to soothe pain and promote the progress of abscesses when pus was forming. Cod liver oil was also ordered in bulk. It was used as a dietary supplement, as a tonic, and in the treatment of tuberculosis. In 1862 the Infirmary used 215 gallons in a year, and in 1878 seventy-six gallons cost over £14 for one quarter. Both commodities caused problems, however. In 1856 it was reported that 'the tap of the Cod Liver Oil cask had been eaten off by the Rats' and that tin vessels were to be used for both the oil and the linseed meal. The problem was explained by an order several years later that the stable should be used for its 'legitimate purpose', and that a suitable alternative place be provided for the drugs.

Alcohol was commonly used as a medical treatment until late in the nineteenth century, either as the basis for medicines, or prescribed neat as a 'stimulant' which was thought to strengthen the patient. Thus whisky, brandy, gin, sherry and port were bought in copious amounts. Such treatment was often cheaper than drugs, and probably often as effective.

In 1878 a *Pharmacopœia* of remedies used by the Infirmary was published which gave more information on the drugs used there. The prescriptions, in Latin, included eye drops and washes, gargles, 'Injectiones' or internal treatments for venereal diseases, lotions for skin complaints and infestations, pills, and mixtures, of which the majority were for stomach complaints, some were for coughs or chest problems, and some contained opium for pain relief. Many of these remedies survived with little change into the twentieth century. Although the prescriptions were for a wide range of diseases, the predominance of those for digestive disorders shows how widespread were such complaints, largely because of the poor diet of the working-class patients. It also suggests that the Infirmary was being used, at least by outpatients, for the treatment of many minor complaints.

Surgery was also rarely mentioned in the Minute Books, except when difficulties arose. More was revealed in the local newspapers, especially in inquest reports of accident cases. These illustrated the difficulties of surgeons faced with amputations and other major injuries in the period before antisepsis, and the risks of anaesthesia before effective methods of patient assessment were available. The first use of chloroform was reported in detail, only three weeks after the first published account of its use in 1847. An account in the *Bradford Observer* stressed the success of the operation and the competence of the surgeons, but another account, giving the date as 1850, claimed that the administration of chloroform,

> ... *was made by a surgeon who was himself in terror of the supposed danger of the experiment and in the presence of a body of doctors who witnessed it in an atmosphere of awed suspense.*

The account also mentions a staff of four untrained nurses 'one or more of whom frequently had to be carried to bed in a condition of drunkenness', but the original source for these observations is unknown. Two operations for lithotomy, to remove stones from the bladder, were similarly reported in detail in the *Observer*, one of which was,

> ... *performed in the presence of several gentlemen, among whom was the Dean of Ripon ...these operations were performed while the patients were under the influence of chloroform.*

Whilst patients benefited from anaesthesia, conditions in the operating room were not always ideal. In 1853 it was filled with smoke from the fireplace, 'so as almost to prevent the use of the room', whilst three years later the surgical instruments had rusted from damp in the room, and were to be stored in baize-lined

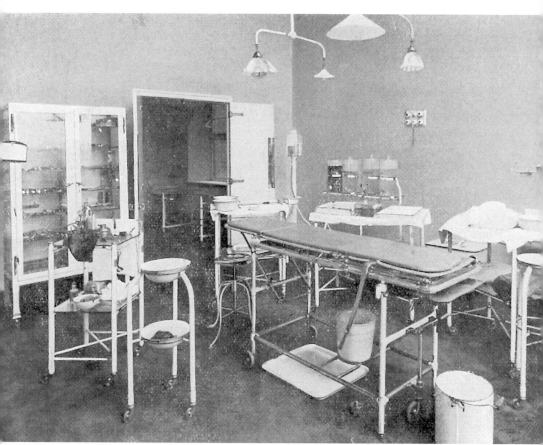

Figure 7. An operating theatre. *Bradford Infirmary Report, 1910.*

drawers. The middle of the room was later floored with oilcloth, and six chairs provided for onlookers. (Figure 7)

There is no mention of the use of antiseptic procedures in the Infirmary until fifteen years after the technique was first described. In 1880 two successful cases of the removal of ovarian cysts were described by an Infirmary surgeon, who stated that he had used 'strict antiseptic precautions'. Another doctor said, however, that surgeons 'generally preferred a special house rather than a hospital for these cases, to avoid unfavourable surroundings'.

Although conditions for surgery undoubtedly improved, bandages were still made from old linen donated to the Infirmary, and in 1892 the need for 'atmospheric purity' in the operating theatre led to expensive alterations. By the end of the century the number of operations had increased from 172 in 1886, to 853 in 1900. Although many of these were minor procedures, they no doubt represented the relief of a great deal of suffering for the Infirmary patients.

Nursing Care

The Infirmary Committee Minutes give the impression that their nurses were uneducated and immoral women, but this reflects the fact that the committees were dealing with problems when they arose, but made little comment when affairs progressed smoothly.

The first mention of a nurse was in 1834. By 1850 there was also an upper or head nurse, and in 1851 there were three nurses, all middle-aged widows or married women. Although in 1851 the Board had decided that 'three well-qualified nurses' were required, they advertised only for 'A Person of Experience and good Character' with wages at £15 a year, and the following year only for 'an Efficient nurse'. In 1863 two trained nurses were appointed, but by 1865 it was suggested that 'superior nurses, such as are to be obtained from the training institutions of London or Liverpool' were needed. The number of nurses rose from three, plus two night nurses, in 1861, to ten in 1871, their ages ranging from twenty to sixty-two. Shortly afterwards the quality of nursing began to improve with the development of nurse training within the Infirmary, which began when there was difficulty in obtaining a supply of efficient nurses from elsewhere. In 1891 there were nine nurses and two probationers, and by the end of the century ten ward sisters and thirty-seven nurses and probationers. The majority of these were probationers, fifteen of them in their first year of training.

There were many problems during the period before trained nurses were appointed, some of which arose from lack of supervision and training. Nurses were reprimanded for 'their carelessness in emptying the Dressing Boxes, Poultices, etc down the Water Closets' and for leaving 'the poultice cloths and dirtied sheets as taken from the patients in the water closets for a week at a time instead of taking them to the wash house daily'. That they received little medical instruction is shown in an inquest report in the *Observer*. A nurse gave evidence that turpentine cloths had been used to treat inflammation, but this was corrected by the doctor who stated that they were used for pain relief. He added that 'a nurse's knowledge is necessarily most superficial'. Despite this lack of basic knowledge which might have improved patient care, the nurse was spoken of by other patients 'in the most kindly terms'. She was described as 'an

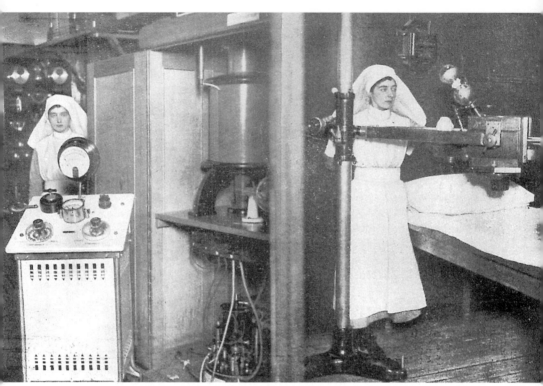

Figure 8. Nurses in the electrical department. *Bradford Royal Infirmary: an epitome, 1912.*

old Scotch woman, ever full of sympathy and kindness for the patients' (Figure 8).

However, other evidence shows that nurses were dismissed for drunkenness, including one who accepted brandy from a patient, for insubordination to doctors, immoral conduct with doctors and others, immoral conduct and theft combined, and neglect of patients, a complaint which was also made at an inquest in 1881, but which was deemed to be unfounded. The nurses were not entirely to blame for their behaviour; the Infirmary matrons were not always above criticism, and more than one was dismissed for mismanagement and other faults. One, whose 'health has not proved equal to the duties that have devolved upon her' was taken to an asylum after less than six months. In a very public confrontation between the resident medical officers and the matron in 1870 it was stated that the matron

*had made use of most unbecoming language to the nurses, and by false
statements had endeavoured to injure them'.*

She was described by a subscriber as lacking 'judgement, truthfulness, benevolence and tact.'

But despite such difficulties, the nurses were sometimes singled out for their good work, both by the public for their 'tenderest nursing' and by the governors in the form of wage increases for long service and having 'given full satisfaction'. The development of professional nursing generally ended serious complaints about their conduct.

In 1892 a patient said that,

*...the nurses were always very kind to us. They have stingy, irritable
folks to deal with sometimes, but I have seldom heard any complaints,
and only then from persons who ...had a propensity for grumbling
which was ever ready to assert itself.*

If the nurses had their faults, so did their managers and their patients. But despite their failings, they were from the same class as the patients, and perhaps had more sympathy for them, and a better understanding of them than any other hospital staff.

Conclusion

Patients themselves were rarely articulate enough to describe or complain about hospital conditions, and only the visitors from the Ladies Committee were concerned with promoting the comfort of the patients. Thus there are few records which directly contribute to our knowledge of what it was like to be a patient in the Infirmary in the nineteenth century. However, although lack of money was always a problem in Bradford, there is no evidence that patient conditions were any worse than other similar institutions of the time. Compared to the environment in which most of the poor lived, the Infirmary provided care, comfort, and a good diet, which all contributed to the patients' eventual return to health.

Sources

Bradford Infirmary Annual Reports, 1855 - 1901.
Bradford Infirmary Board of Management and Committee Minute Books, 1825 - 1901.
Bradford Medico-Chirurgical Society Minute Books, 1874 - 1904.
Bradford Observer, 1834 - 1901.
Census Reports, 1851 - 1891.
Forshaw, T.G. comp. *Bradford Infirmary and Dispensary Pharmacopœia.* Bradford, 1878.
Sixth Report to the Medical Department of the Privy Council on the Hospitals of the United Kingdom.,
1864 [Bristowe and Holmes].
'Within the Hospitals: Bradford Infirmary,' *The Hospital*, 1892. (17 December), pp.189-190.

11. James Burnley, 'The Saunterer's Satchel', and the Bradford Literati

by Stephen Wade

ONE OF THE MOST FASCINATING STUDIES in local history relates to questions of region and belonging. We cannot resist this pull of curiosity about how and why our ancestors expressed their identity through such aspects of popular culture as local dialect literature, songs, parades, concerts and so on. In the Victorian period this curiosity is perhaps more easily explained. After all, this was the period of turmoil and rapid social change in which issues of class difference became more acute and more significant.

In the late nineteenth century there was a widespread flowering of local writing, often in the vernacular, and sometimes in remarkably original and vibrant dialect. It was a period in which local and regional publishing were burgeoning, and it was not difficult for an earnest middle class amateur poet to bring his or her work into print. The sense of local belonging was mediated to all classes, however, and the literature of the time shows this awareness on the part of the publishers that they should cater for all tastes.

It is in Bradford, perhaps more than in any other Victorian city, that the literary culture around the new aspirations to read and write both high quality literature and popular narratives, is apparent. There are many reasons for this: the influx of German immigrants who brought their love of higher cultural pursuits, the appeal of a bohemian, cosmopolitan culture to the new middle class; and most of all, to the energy of individuals. In Bradford, there was a 'nest of singing birds' gathered around various clubs, coffee houses and societies, and a key figure in this was the writer and journalist, James Burnley (Figure 1).

The time was right for such a figure to emerge. The local civic pride was developing in step with the legislation for incorporation (Bradford being made a County Borough in 1889) and with the

Figure 1. James Burnley.
Bradford Libraries.

Figure 2. St George's Hall, 1873. *Brear's Guide to Bradford, 1873.*

Figure 3. St George's Hall. *Bradford Libraries*

establishment of literary and philosophical societies such as those thriving in Leeds and Hull in the mid-Victorian years. As Asa Briggs puts it when comparing Bradford with Leeds: Bradford was the first of the two communities to sponsor a handsome new public building which was designed to 'elevate' taste and meet the 'cultural needs of a business metropolis'[1] and also, with St George's Hall, Briggs points out, 'What happened inside it was to raise the tone of society also'[2] (Figures 2 and 3).

A fundamental part of this Bradford culture, though, was in the people, not simply in the buildings and grand public gestures of politicians. Writing was becoming a booming local cultural product, offering outlets for the mediocre enthusiast and the genuine creative spirit. James Burnley was at the heart of this, as editor, poet, comedian and serious social commentator. As Ian Dewhirst has recently pointed out, the authors being published could range from clergymen to anonymous operatives on the factory floor.[3] Burnley came on the literary scene with a few poems and a knowledge of the London theatre in the 1860s, and soon became involved with the group of writers around the *Bradford Observer* and *Bradford Review*.

Several writers of later years have commented on the cultural richness and diversity of late Victorian Bradford, so it is not difficult to imagine the context in which Burnley thrived. W. Riley, for instance, in his autobiography, notes:

> *Good reference libraries were close at hand; good lectures were available; cultured men and women were ready to stimulate and encourage the serious student. As I recall to mind the opportunities that then presented themselves I appropriate to myself the well-known line of Wordsworth: 'Bliss was it in that dawn to be alive'.* [4]

Peter Holdsworth has pointed out the importance of this setting for the young J.B.Priestley, commenting that '...in his youth Bradford was... culturally dynamic. Theatre, literary pursuits, sport and the visual arts thrived alongside a host of societies.'[5]

But in the earlier period, when Burnley arrived, there was a notable difference to the more institutionalised developments of the *fin de siàcle* Bradford. The writing was more directly comprehensive, aware of working men who wanted good literature as well as supplying the needs of the articulate, leisured middle class who wanted theatre reviews and bookish *belles lettres*. Burnley had such a wide range of writing ability that he could fit in with the drinkers and workers at Thomas Nicholson's eating house in Kirkgate, talking to almanac writers and singers, but also dine with the large-scale entrepreneurs, whose lives he was to write about in his best-selling book, *The Romance of Modern Industry* (1886).

Burnley was born in Shipley in 1842, and began his long publishing career with a volume of poems, *Idonia and other poems* (1869) but his talents extended to other compositions such as plays, sketches, travel writing, fiction and journalism. He became most celebrated as 'The Saunterer', the man who produced the almanac *The Saunterer's Satchel* throughout the last decades of the century, and also well-known for his 'sketches' books - *Phases of Bradford Life* (1871) and *West Riding Sketches* (1875). These two books illustrate the special qualities that made Burnley central to this Bradford literary culture; his mix of serious commentary and understanding humour, and his ability to embrace the range of cultural reference from folklore to modern industrial processes. In fact, his most successful books celebrated the woollen industry and the wider Victorian preoccupations with 'rags to riches' themes in the age of Samuel Smiles and Self Help. His book, *The History of Wool and Wool-Combing* (1889) appears to have made his name nationally and gave him access to the drawing-rooms of the wealthy.

What defines Burnley's importance to Bradford writing and to the massive success of the whole group of journalists and poets around him is his local publishing achievements, largely with the founding of *The Yorkshireman* in 1875, initially as a monthly. In later years, as one memoirist puts it, he resided in London 'and made a host of friends among the leading literati of the metropolis'.[6] In other words, here we have a writer who was one of a class who succeeded in the wake of the huge ocean liner that was dominating the literature of the age: the tugs and supply-boats of the scene. Burnley was very much the 'bookman' of the time, as depicted by Walter Besant:

> *...a good steady man of letters... this man... goes to his study every morning as regularly as a barrister goes to chambers. He finds on his desk two or three books waiting for review, a manuscript sent for his opinion, a book of his own to go on with...* [7]

But for the student of Yorkshire writing, his importance is illustrated when we look closer at the nature of his almanac, *The Saunterer's Satchel*. Here was a publication that stands out in its time. The almanac, as established in the working-class author tradition, notably in Barnsley, Halifax and Leeds, had been primarily a calendar with anniversaries, a vehicle for local advertisers (notably of patent medicines) and perhaps the first type of publication supplying that local dialect verse and narrative that provided sustenance for the

Figure 4. Cover of *Clock Almanack*. *Watmoughs.*

local and civic pride so foregrounded in the literature and art of the period. The most celebrated almanac, John Hartley's *Clock*, exemplifies this (Figure 4). The average issue contained humour, anecdotes and rhymes, all very much to the popular taste and similar to the material in demand for penny readings and for dialect recitals such as those given by Ben Preston following afternoon tea and Bible classes (Figure 5). The success of Penny Readings was obviously a factor. London publishers were producing hardback volumes for these readings by the 1870s (notably Frederick Warne).

Burnley's *Satchel* is something else completely. A typical issue would contain a preface with a chatty tone, a comic drama set in Yorkshire, songs and rhymes in dialect and in standard English, and fiction. Burnley also introduced an Answers to Correspondents column and local news items. These were to continue in the more ambitious *Yorkshireman*. But what defines the difference between the *Satchel* and its competitors are the literary allusions and parodies it included. For instance, we have 'A Kersmas Tale - *Not* by Munchausen' and rhymes 'not by Poe'. In one rhyme, 'Sing the Song of the Fleece' Burnley calls the sections of the poem 'fyttes', so referring to medieval forms. All this indicates that his readership was a mix of the people who simply wanted racy and farcical tales and the middle-class aspirants who read 'good literature' and would know a parody when they read it. Even more impressive was the local and topographical nature of the references squeezed into the rhymes, such as, 'Of Alpacas superb in which Salts are investors/Of the fleece of the goat from the wilds of Angora/Which makes such sweet dresses for Florry and Dora' (Figure 6).

The contents and tone of the *Satchel* indicate

Figure 5. Ben Preston, poet. *Bradford Libraries.*

that Burnley was keenly aware of the readership, and that the keynote was entertainment. Repeatedly, his prefaces stress the content as 'puns quite a sea for jokers facetious to dabble in' and 'stories fantastic and stories sarcastic'. His aim is always to promote writers 'who've been rangers in regions sublime; whose pens, by heaven nourished, give forth grand thoughts for all time.' In a remarkable typescript written by Burnley late in life, *Literary Recollections of Bradford 1870-1890*, he summarises the groups of literati around Bradford at the time. These would be the writers who supplied copy to the whole range of magazines, almanacs and newspapers of the area. Burnley lists the main figures:

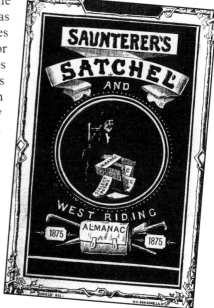

Figure 6. Cover of *Saunterer's Satchel*. *Watmoughs.*

> *...and into this haunt would occasionally stray for mind-communion John James, the historian of Bradford, for he frequently visited the town he had made famous; Robert Storey, the Craven poet, Ben Preston, Stephen Fawcett, James Hird and others, with mine host Nicholson, Smoking his long pipe, presiding.*[8]

In his *Phases of Bradford Life*, in which Burnley collected many of his local writings, he has a piece on 'Coffee House Life' and this makes clear exactly what it was like to be involved in this 'mind-communion':

> *Here in Bradford there still exist coffee-rooms where discussions on the topics of the day constitute a special feature, and where almost any night may be heard debates equal in vigour, if not in ability, to any heard within the walls of the House of Commons.*[9]

He writes of 'Straycock's Temperance Hotel' in a dingy court of Kirkgate, and has gentle fun at the expense of the crowd of regulars. Even more pastiche and satire are injected into a sketch called 'Barnacle's Evening Party', in which the Pickwick Club is echoed. The guest list is an exaggeration of the range of writers who perhaps really gather in the Bradford circle of the time. They include such worthies as 'Abimelech Flavonius de Smithkins, the great local author

and historian of Wibsey Slack' and 'Mr. Silvanio, the tragedian' (Figure 7). Barnacles provides his guests with a selection of literature at the party, and this includes: 'Long Yarns by an Old Spinner - a most amusing volume' and 'Looming in the Distance - a three-volume novel by the author of *Fell'd at last.*'

There were some remarkable characters in the circle around Burnley, and their enthusiasm and high level of literary appreciation is typified by J. Arthur Binns, whom Burnley describes thus:

But in those years of the late sixties and early seventies he was

Figure 7. John James, historian. *Bradford Libraries.*

a man of some leisure and disclosed to me a mind better stored with literary knowledge than that of any men I have ever known... He was chairman of the library committee of the old Mechanics' Institute. He knew the poets so thoroughly that he had many of their best pieces literally off by heart. He could recite the whole of Pope's Essay on Man, and reel off poems and stanzas from Shelley... [10]

To Bradford generally he was known as the President of the Third Equitable Building Society (Figure 8).

A volume edited by another Bradford literary man, Charles Forshaw, *The Poets of Bingley, Keighley and Haworth* (1891) gives an insight into the whole community of writers of all shades: poetasters, neo-Romantics, hack journalists and wealthy amateurs. (Figure 9) The volume was financed by subscription, and the list of subscribers reflects the sheer diversity of creative people around Burnley. There are no fewer than twenty-nine local publications listed, largely poetry collections and anthologies of local writing. Burnley himself, in his contribution to the book (on James Hird, Figure 10) says something that defines the spirit behind this Bradford literary circle:

Figure 8. J.A. Binns, writer. *Bradford Libraries.*

Figure 9. C.F. Foreshaw, writer and editor. *Bradford Libraries.*

As Mr Hird advanced to manhood he forced himself into a better career than the mill had offered him, and by dint

Figure 10. James Hird, poet. *Bradford Libraries.*

of self-culture and perseverance was able to take up a position... that yielded him greater opportunities... for the expansion of his mind and the exercise of his poetic gifts.[11]

A remarkable feature of this literary culture was that, as time went on, links were made with other towns. John Hartley was involved, and when a Yorkshire Literary Union was formed in April 1870, there was a notable insistence on the importance of a body of 'Yorkshire Literature' forming an important part of the consciousness of how people belonged to this region, with a sense of place and identity that sustained a massive publication programme for decades (Figure 11). Burnley insists on the general camaraderie in addition to literary matters. He writes that

It must not be imagined that the Bradford writers did not chum together socially as well as in literary matters.... There was a strain of Bohemianism about some of us....

He clearly hankered for a mix of café society and serious literary production, and his works reflect this diversity.

As the focal achievement in all this endeavour was undoubtedly the writing of dialect literature with an intention of treating it as more than a novelty, it has to be stressed that the dramas, tales and poems in the *Yorkshireman* and in the *Satchel* represent a genuine attempt to depict the authentic domestic and labouring lives of people in the area

Figure 11. John Hartley, journalist. *Bradford Libraries.*

(Figure 12). The drama owes a lot to the London tradition of burlesque as written by such satirists as Cruikshank, but there is not always an avoidance of sentimentality in the writing. When the realism is successful, there is an attempt to present the vernacular with care in terms of phonetic accuracy, giving the writing a genuine feel. It also creates the shared humour that a magazine constructs

Figure 12. Detail from the cover of *Saunterer's Satchel.* *Bradford Libraries.*

with reader and writer, as initiated by Addison and Steele with the early eighteenth century *Spectator*. After all, this was the era in which dialect writers were beginning to attract large audiences and had reading circuits and substantial volumes of their work published. Edwin Waugh (1817-1890) typifies this, surviving as a full-time writer. The tradition of selling pamphlets and booklets in the streets was still continued. The establishment of the English Dialect Society in 1877 suggests just how much of an expansion of interest in this literature had developed by the time of Burnley's publications.

In 1889 Burnley stepped up to become an amateur sociologist and business correspondent. In this he moved from historian of the folk culture to the celebration of success, of the puritan work ethic and of the transformation effected by wealth and social status. The basis of his enquiry into the success of men such as Titus Salt, Cunliffe Lister and Isaac Holden is that 'Romance and industry have long been regarded in the popular mind as things apart' and that 'The imagination is always impressed by stories of men who have carved their way from obscurity to wealth...'.

Burnley's work in Bradford has a greater significance than has been given. As a writer, propagandist for social progress and the amelioration of man through work and cultural fulfilment, Burnley surely deserves to be re-read. His writings provide valuable evidence of important social and cultural history; but far more important than this is his place in the chronicles of both an emerging working class interest in literature and in the middle class acquisition of the 'higher culture' of the upper classes. All this came at a time when English literature was only just in the process of becoming recognised as a subject with meaning and status. But it was the Bradford setting, and its unique contributions to the new publishing enterprises that gave Burnley his real break as a writer:

As he put it in the introduction to *West Riding Sketches*:

> *In the West Riding... the old and new clash together so indiscriminately, the prose and the poetry intermingle so curiously, that it requires one to be 'native' and 'to the manner born' to distinguish the lines of demarcation.*

Burnley was very much the creation of the emergence of regional consciousness born of civic pride, and the writers in his circle certainly understood that Yorkshire was an entity, as part of a concept of 'The North', that it was also a state of mind, and that it needed a literature of its own, largely to counteract the stereotypes given by London writers.

In helping to cultivate these things in and around Bradford, Burnley was more than simply a jobbing literary man. He and his Bradford friends never produced anything that did not have its foundation in an affection for the city. In his final words of his recollections, he says:

> *Of course, every decade does not give Bradford a Ben Preston, or a Broughton, or a Robbins... still, with the encouraging examples of those twenty years to look back upon, there ought to be incentive enough to budding literary talent to put forth its highest endeavours in advancing the literary reputation of this good old town.* [12]

How right he was. In the decade after Burnley's time there, a young J.B. Priestley was talking shop in the Swan Arcade, and reading the almanacs.

A study of James Burnley's achievement in Bradford surely confirms to the literary historian that he should perhaps look more closely at how regional writing did more than simply ape a Dickens or a Trollope. The careers of the whole circle around him illustrate that there was much more to them as writers than merely a talking shop of dilettantes.

Notes and References

1 Asa Briggs, *Victorian Cities* (Penguin, 1990) p. 143.
2 *ibid.* p. 153.
3 See Ian Dewhirst, 'The Doctor, The Druggist and relieving Officer: Some Haworth and District Writers of the Brontë Era' in Robert Duckett (ed.) *Brontë Society Transactions* Vol. 23, Part 1, April 1998 pp. 63-70.
4 W. Riley, *Sunset Reflections* (Herbert Jenkins, 1957) p. 57.
5 Peter Holdsworth, *The Rebel Tyke: Bradford and J.B. Priestley* (Bradford Libraries) 1994 p. 19.
6 See William Andrews' introduction to Burnley's poetry in Charles H. Forshaw's *The Poets of Keighley, Bingley and Haworth* (Thornton and Pearson: Bradford) 1891 pp. 42-43.
7 See John Gross' account of the bookman's life in *The Rise and fall of the Man Of Letters* (Penguin, 1977) chapter seven particularly.
8 James Burnley, *Literary Recollections of Bradford* 1870-1890 ms. Held in Bradford Central Libraries, Local History section.
9 *ibid.*
10 *ibid.*
11 In C. Forshaw, *The Poets of Keighley, Bingley and Haworth,* p.108.
12 James Burnley, *Literary Recollections,* p.37.

Checklist of works by Burnley

The main sources for his earlier life and work are his own manuscript pages kept in Bradford City Libraries: *Literary Recollections of Bradford 1870-1890.* Ref. B792 BUR

A. Books
Biskra and the Desert: a record of a tour in Algeria in the year 1885 (Bradford: privately printed) 1906.
Fetters. A comedy-drama in a prologue and three acts (Bradford: Burnley) 1876.

The History of Wool and Wool-combing (Bradford: Sampson, Low) 1889.
Idonia and Other Poems (London: Longmans) 1869.
Looking for the Dawn: a tale of the West Riding. (London: Simpkin, Marshall) 1874.
Phases of Bradford Life: a series of pen and ink sketches (London: Simpkin Marshall) 1871.
The Romance of Invention; vignettes from the annals of industry and science. (London: Cassell) 1886.
Sir Titus Salt and George Moore (London: Cassell) 1891.
Two Sides of the Atlantic (London: Simpkin, Marshall) 1890.
West Riding Sketches (London: Hodder and Stoughton) 1875.

B. Publications from journalism: collected
A Bradford Institution (Bradford Mechanics Institute) 1875.
Busy Bradford: its development and past and present notabilities London, *The Magazine*, 1903.
The Streets of Bradford, Photocopies of cuttings from the *Bradford Observer*, 1883. A series of articles
dealing with local streets and their development.

C. Work in anthologies
Essays on local authors in Charles Forshaw (ed.) *The Poets of Keighley, Bingley and Howarth*
(Bradford: Thornton and Pearson) 1891.

N.B. In this work, there is also a biographical profile of Burnley by William Andrews (pp. 42-43).

D. Almanacs
Editor of *The Saunterer's Satchel* (Bradford: from 1888 to 1910). (Figure 12).

CONTRIBUTORS

Despite suffering William Blake's stereotype of the North as a land of 'dark, satanic mills', **Bob Duckett** arrived in Bradford in 1974 for a job interview one sunny spring day to find cherry blossom in the grounds of City Hall, glorious architecture, and glimpses of moorland from his future place of work. So he stayed, and now lives with Pam, his librarian wife, in Baildon. They have two sons and a daughter.

Born during the war, Bob came to Bradford via a childhood in Enfield and Croydon, universities in Glasgow and Leicester, and jobs in Bangor (Wales) and Birmingham. He is active in the Brontë and J.B. Priestley Societies, The Library Association, regularly contributes chapters and articles to books and journals, plays chess for UNISON, and has a daytime job as Bradford's Reference Librarian. His ambition is to find time to write a chapter for *Aspects of Bradford*.

1. RANDOM REVERIE: MEMORIES OF AN IMPRESSIONABLE CHILD

David Hird is a native Bradfordian, born in Little Horton. In 1963 he entered local government in the Town Clerk's Department of the City of Bradford where he specialised in election and electoral law, transferring to the borough of Brighouse as Deputy Returning Officer in 1968 and Wakefield City Council as Deputy Returning Officer in 1970. On the reorganisation of local government in 1974 David became Elections, Electoral Registration and Deputy Returning Officer to the successor authority, Wakefield City M.D.C. In 1982 he resigned to take a small country inn at the head of Wharfedale. In 1989 he returned to local government with Craven District Council, specialising in financial law, until the welcome embrace of premature retirement presented itself in 1995, and he hit the ground running! He continues to live in upper Wharfedale, pursuing his interests in industrial archaeology, local history, early transport generally and the development of communication routes and systems.

2. LIFE IN MID-EIGHTEENTH CENTURY BRADFORD

Elvira Willmott graduated in history at University College, London, and qualified as a librarian, working in London and Dorset before coming to Yorkshire in 1970 to work for the West Riding County Library Service. From 1974 she was in charge of local history at Bradford Central Library until her retirement in 1996. In 1986 Elvira obtained an MA degree at Huddersfield Polytechnic with a thesis about Bradford in the mid-eighteenth century. In addition to local history her interests include family history and music.

3. SCHOOL DAYS (1931-1944)

Arnold Kellett. On leaving Carlton school, Arnold Kellett served in the Intelligence Corps, mostly in the Far East, then studied at the Sorbonne and the University of Liverpool, where he took a first class degree in French language and literature. He then taught at Ashville College, Harrogate, and King James' School, Knaresborough, where he became head of modern languages, taking early retirement in 1983. Dr Kellett has twice served as Mayor of Knaresborough, and is a well-known authority on the town's history, having been awarded the Yorkshire History Prize in 1988 for his research establishing that King John held the first known Royal Maundy in Knaresborough in 1210. He has published several books on local history and Yorkshire dialect, and is editor of the Transactions of the Yorkshire Dialect Society. He traces both his involvement in dialect and Methodism to a happy upbringing in Wibsey, where he met his wife Pat, who presides with him over four children and fifteen grandchildren.

4. METHODISM IN BRADFORD

Dr Simon Valentine is Head of Religious Studies at Bradford Grammar School and an Associate Lecturer at the University of Bradford. He possesses degrees in Law and Theology and a Masters degree and Doctorate in Ecclesiastical History. He has numerous articles published in newspapers and journals and a major biography on John Bennet and the origin of Methodism and the Evangelical Revival in England published by Scarecrow Press in 1998. He is a Methodist Local Preacher . His hobbies include fell walking and photography. He is married to Irene and has two sons, John and Daniel.

5. FULL CIRCLE AT ILKLEY: HYDROTHERAPY TO HOUSECRAFT

Patricia Brown was born in Rochdale in 1946. She was educated at Heybrook School and Rochdale Secondary Technical School before being accepted at Ilkley College of Housecraft in 1963, at the age of seventeen, to train as a teacher. She has taught in several Rochdale schools both full and part-time before moving first to Lawefield Middle School and then to Horbury School, Wakefield. Here she was Head of Department teaching Food and Textiles

Technology and child development prior to her early retirement in 1995. Since then she has qualified as an aromatherapist at Dewsbury College. She also enjoys writing local history articles for various publications. She is married with three grown-up children, several cats and a rescue dog called Fred.

---

6. HAWORTH CHURCHYARD: WHO WERE THEY?

Ann Dinsdale has lived most of her life in West Yorkshire. She is the librarian of the Brontë Parsonage Museum at Haworth, home of the world's largest collection of Brontëana. She is also involved with organising exhibitions and assisting scholars. She lectures and writes on aspects of the Brontës' lives and social conditions in mid-nineteenth century Haworth. Her book, *Old Haworth*, a collection of historic views of Haworth, was published in 1999.

---

7. IMPRISONED FOR THEIR CONSCIENCE: KEIGHLEY'S ANTI-VACCINATION PROTEST

Pauline Barfield, Bradford born and bred, was educated at Grange Girls Grammar School. Starting work for Bradford Libraries at the age of sixteen in the Darley Street Lending Library, she worked in several branch libraries before returning to work in the Social Sciences Department in the newly opened Central Library, Princes Way. Pauline was appointed Reference Librarian at Keighley in 1997. She is married with two grown-up daughters. At the time of writing she is building on a lifelong interest in local history by studying for a Certificate in Higher Education in Yorkshire Studies at Bradford University.

8. The Glory of Lister Park: A Century of Enjoyment

Peter Shutt was born in Heaton in 1926, and was educated at Bradford's Belle Vue Grammar School. After working in Lister Park for a time, he left to continue his education at Leeds University. He joined the West Riding Education Service, eventually becoming a Principal Officer with the Metropolitan Borough of Calderdale Education Authority. On retirement, Peter pursued a career in art and has exhibited work in London and New York in addition to galleries throughout Yorkshire. He is one of the founder members of the Yorkshire Watercolour Society and runs residential leisure painting courses. Other interests are gardening, photography and walking, particularly in the Lake District, winter and summer. Peter lives in Bailiff Bridge, Brighouse.

9. H.L.B.L. and the Fountain Brewery

Tony Avis grew up in rural Norfolk and in 1956 he came to work at Hammond's Fountain Brewery in Bradford's Manchester Road, soon becoming Company Secretary. After Hammond's (or United Breweries as it had become) Tony worked for Bentley and Shaw at Lockwood in Kirklees, and for their successors, Bass plc. He is the author of several books including *The Brewing Industry, 1950 - 1990* and *Timothy Bentley; Master Brewer of Yorkshire*. Tony lives in Ilkley.

10. A Patient's Lot at the Westgate Infirmary

Christine Alvin spent her working life as a librarian, mostly in the Bradford area. This included ten years in the Postgraduate Medical Library at the Bradford Royal Infirmary, where she first came across the records of the old Infirmary which are now held at the Wakefield headquarters of the West Yorkshire Archives. Since taking early retirement she has undertaken a PhD  thesis at Bradford University on the subject of Medical Treatment and Care in Nineteenth Century Bradford. Christine lives in Thackley.

11. James Burnley, *The Saunterer's Satchel*, and the Bradford Literati

Stephen Wade was born in Leeds and now lectures in Huddersfield, where he specialises in creative writing at the university, returning 'home' after a long spell teaching in Lincolnshire. His interest in Yorkshire writing and writers goes back many years, and his own poetry and fiction are often concerned with West Riding life. His collections, *Churwell Poems, Exits and Entrances* and *Adult*  *Education* all concern relationships, work and play in Yorkshire. He is currently working on a monograph about the life of James Burnley for the 1890s Society. Almost all of his writing is concerned with versions of region and belonging, and its expression in art. He also writes freelance journalism and gives regular readings and workshops throughout the northern counties.

INDEX - PLACES